TWO
BY
GEORGE C. WOLFE

TWO
BY
GEORGE C. WOLFE

THE COLORED MUSEUM
&
SPUNK
Three Tales
by Zora Neale Hurston
Adapted by
George C. Wolfe

The Fireside Theatre

GARDEN CITY, NEW YORK

THE
COLORED
MUSEUM

The Colored Museum had its world premiere at the Crossroads Theatre Company on 26 March 1986. Rich Khan was the Executive Director; Lee Richardson, the Artistic Director who directed the following cast:

Arnold Bankston
Olivia Virgil Harper
Robert Jason
Myra Taylor
Vickilyn Reynolds
and Natasha Durant as THE LITTLE GIRL

Brian Martin designed the set; Nancy Konrardy, the costumes; Hope Clarke, the choreography; William H. Grant III, the lighting; and Rob Gorton, the sound. Kysia Bostic composed original music; Daryl Waters directed the musical and vocal arrangements. Kenneth Johnson was the Production Stage Manager. Anton Nelessen did the slide projections.

The Colored Museum previewed at Joseph Papp's New York Shakespeare Festival on 7 October 1986. It opened on 2 November 1986 with L. Kenneth Richardson directing the following cast ensemble:

Loretta Devine
Tommy Hollis
Reggie Montgomery
Vickilyn Reynolds
Danitra Vance

Kysia Bostic was the composer/arranger; Brian Martin created the scenery, Nancy L. Konrardy, the costumes, and William H. Grant III, the lighting; Hope Clarke was the choreographer; Daryl Waters, the musical director; Anton Nelessen did the slide projections.

The Cast: An ensemble of five, two men and three women, all black, who perform all the characters that inhabit the exhibits.*

The Stage: White walls and recessed lighting. A starkness befitting a museum where the myths and madness of black/Negro/colored Americans are stored.

Built into the wall are a series of small panels, doors, revolving walls, and compartments from which actors can retrieve key props and make quick entrances.

A revolve is used, which allows for quick transitions from one exhibit to the next.

Music: All of the music for the show should be pre-recorded. Only the drummer, who is used in *Git on Board,* and then later in *Permutations* and *The Party,* is live.

THERE IS NO INTERMISSION

---

* A LITTLE GIRL, seven to twelve years old, is needed for a walk-on part in *Lala's Opening.*

The Exhibits

Git on Board
Cookin' with Aunt Ethel
The Photo Session
Soldier with a Secret
The Gospel According to Miss Roj
The Hairpiece
The Last Mama-on-the-Couch Play
Symbiosis
Lala's Opening
Permutations
The Party

Characters

Git on Board
MISS PAT

Cookin' with Aunt Ethel
AUNT ETHEL

The Photo Session
GIRL
GUY

Soldier with a Secret
JUNIE ROBINSON

The Gospel According to Miss Roj
MISS ROJ
WAITER

The Hairpiece
THE WOMAN
JANINE
LAWANDA

The Last Mama-on-the-Couch Play
NARRATOR
MAMA
WALTER-LEE-BEAU-WILLIE-JONES
LADY IN PLAID
MEDEA JONES

Symbiosis
THE MAN
THE KID

Lala's Opening
LALA LAMAZING GRACE
ADMONIA
FLO'RANCE
THE LITTLE GIRL

Permutations
NORMAL JEAN REYNOLDS

The Party
TOPSY WASHINGTON
MISS PAT
MISS ROJ
LALA LAMAZING GRACE
THE MAN *(from Symbiosis)*

Git on Board

(*Blackness. Cut by drums pounding. Then slides, rapidly flashing before us. Images we've all seen before, of African slaves being captured, loaded onto ships, tortured. The images flash, flash, flash. The drums crescendo. Blackout. And then lights reveal* MISS PAT, *frozen. She is black, pert, and cute. She has a flip to her hair and wears a hot pink mini-skirt stewardess uniform.*)

(*She stands in front of a curtain which separates her from an off-stage cockpit.*)

(*An electronic bell goes "ding" and* MISS PAT *comes to life, presenting herself in a friendly but rehearsed manner, smiling and speaking as she has done so many times before.*)

MISS PAT: Welcome aboard Celebrity Slaveship, departing the Gold Coast and making short stops at Bahia, Port Au Prince, and Havana, before our final destination of Savannah.

Hi. I'm Miss Pat and I'll be serving you here in Cabin A. We will be crossing the Atlantic at an altitude that's pretty high, so you must wear your shackles at all times.

(*She removes a shackle from the overhead compartment and demonstrates.*)

To put on your shackle, take the right hand and close the metal ring around your left hand like so. Repeat the action using your left hand to secure the right. If you have any trouble bonding yourself, I'd be more than glad to assist.

Once we reach the desired altitude, the Captain will turn off the "Fasten Your Shackle" sign . . . (*She efficiently points out the "FASTEN YOUR SHACKLE" signs on either side of her, which light up.*) . . . allowing you a chance to stretch and dance in the aisles a bit. But otherwise, shackles must be worn at all times.

(*The "Fasten Your Shackles" signs go off.*)

MISS PAT: Also, we ask that you please refrain from call-and-response singing between cabins as that sort of thing can lead to rebellion. And, of course, no drums are allowed on board. Can you repeat after me, "No drums." (*She gets the audience to repeat.*) With a little more enthusiasm, please. "No drums." (*After the audience repeats it.*) That was great!

Once we're airborn, I'll be by with magazines, and earphones can be purchased for the price of your first-born male.

If there's anything I can do to make this middle passage more pleasant, press the little button overhead and I'll be with you faster than you can say, "Go down, Moses." (*She laughs at her "little joke."*) Thanks for flying Celebrity and here's hoping you have a pleasant takeoff.

(*The engines surge, the "Fasten Your Shackle" signs go on, and over-articulate Muzak voices are heard singing as* MISS PAT *pulls down a bucket seat and "shackles-up" for takeoff.*)

VOICES:
GET ON BOARD CELEBRITY SLAVESHIP
GET ON BOARD CELEBRITY SLAVESHIP
GET ON BOARD CELEBRITY SLAVESHIP
THERE'S ROOM FOR MANY A MORE

(*The engines reach an even, steady hum. Just as* MISS PAT *rises and replaces the shackles in the overhead compartment, the faint sound of African drumming is heard.*)

MISS PAT: Hi. Miss Pat again. I'm sorry to disturb you, but someone is playing drums. And what did we just say . . . "No drums." It must be someone in Coach. But we here in Cabin A are not going to respond to those drums. As a matter of fact, we don't

even hear them. Repeat after me. "I don't hear any drums."
(*The audience repeats.*) And "I will not rebel."

(*The audience repeats. The drumming grows.*)

MISS PAT: (*Placating*) OK, now I realize some of us are a bit edgy
after hearing about the tragedy on board The Laughing Mary,
but let me assure you Celebrity has no intention of throwing
you overboard and collecting the insurance. We value you!

(*She proceeds to single out individual passengers/audience members.*)

Why the songs *you* are going to sing in the cotton fields, under
the burning heat and stinging lash, will metamorphose and give
birth to the likes of James Brown and the Fabulous Flames.
And you, yes *you,* are going to come up with some of the best
dances. The best dances! The Watusi! The Funky Chicken! And
just think of what *you* are going to mean to William Faulkner.

All right, so you're gonna have to suffer for a few hundred
years, but from your pain will come a culture so complex. *And,*
with this little item here . . . (*She removes a basketball from
the overhead compartment.*) . . . you'll become millionaires!

(*There is a roar of thunder. The lights quiver and the "Fasten Your
Shackle" signs begin to flash.* MISS PAT *quickly replaces the basketball in the overhead compartment and speaks very reassuringly.*)

MISS PAT: No, don't panic. We're just caught in a little thunder
storm. Now the only way you're going to make it through is if
you abandon your God and worship a new one. So, on the
count of three, let's all sing. One, two, three . . .

NOBODY KNOWS DE TROUBLE I SEEN

Oh, I forgot to mention, when singing, omit the T-H sound.
"The" becomes "de." "They" becomes "dey." Got it? Good!

NOBODY KNOWS . . .
NOBODY KNOWS . . .

Oh, so you don't like that one? Well then let's try another—

SUMMER TIME
AND DE LIVIN' IS EASY

Gershwin. He comes from another oppressed people so he understands.

FISH ARE JUMPIN' . . . come on.
AND DE COTTON IS HIGH.
AND DE COTTON IS . . . Sing, damnit!

(*Lights begin to flash, the engines surge, and there is wild drumming.* MISS PAT *sticks her head through the curtain and speaks with an offstage* CAPTAIN.)

MISS PAT: What?

VOICE OF CAPTAIN (*O.S.*): Time warp!

MISS PAT: Time warp! (*She turns to the audience and puts on a pleasant face.*) The Captain has assured me everything is fine. We're just caught in a little time warp. (*Trying to fight her growing hysteria.*) On your right you will see the American Revolution, which will give the U.S. of A. exclusive rights to your life. And on your left, the Civil War, which means you will vote Republican until F.D.R. comes along. And now we're passing over the Great Depression, which means everybody gets to live the way you've been living. (*There is a blinding flash of light, and an explosion. She screams.*) Ahhhhhhhhh! That was World War I, which is not to be confused with World War II . . . (*There is a larger flash of light, and another explosion.*) . . . Ahhhhh! Which is not to be confused with the Korean War or the Vietnam War, all of which you will play a major role in.

Oh, look, now we're passing over the sixties. Martha and the Vandellas . . . "Julia" with Miss Diahann Carroll . . . Malcom X . . . those five little girls in Alabama . . . Martin Luther King . . . Oh no! The Supremes broke up! (*The drumming intensifies.*) Stop playing those drums! Those drums will be confiscated once we reach Savannah. You can't change history!

You can't turn back the clock! (*To the audience.*) Repeat after
me, I don't hear any drums! I will not rebel! I will not rebel! I
will not re—

(*The lights go out, she screams, and the sound of a plane landing
and screeching to a halt is heard. After a beat, lights reveal a
wasted, disheveled* MISS PAT, *but perky nonetheless.*)

MISS PAT: Hi. Miss Pat here. Things got a bit jumpy back there, but
the Captain has just informed me we have safely landed in Savannah. Please check the overhead before exiting as any baggage you don't claim, we trash.

It's been fun, and we hope the next time you consider travel, it's
with Celebrity.

(*Luggage begins to revolve onstage from offstage left, going past*
MISS PAT *and revolving offstage right. Mixed in with the luggage are
two male slaves and a woman slave, complete with luggage and I.D.
tags around their necks.*)

MISS PAT: (*With routine, rehearsed pleasantness.*)

Have a nice day. Bye bye.
Button up that coat, it's kind of chilly.
Have a nice day. Bye bye.
You take care now.
See you.
Have a nice day.
Have a nice day.
Have a nice day.

Cookin' with Aunt Ethel

(*As the slaves begin to revolve off, a low-down gutbucket blues is heard.* AUNT ETHEL, *a down-home black woman with a bandana on her head, revolves to center stage. She stands behind a big black pot and wears a reassuring grin.*)

AUNT ETHEL: Welcome to "Aunt Ethel's Down-Home Cookin' Show," where we explores the magic and mysteries of colored cuisine.

Today, we gonna be servin' ourselves up some . . . (*She laughs.*) I'm not gonna tell you. That's right! I'm not gonna tell you what it is till after you done cooked it. Child, on "The Aunt Ethel Show" we loves to have ourselves some fun. Well, are you ready? Here goes.

(*She belts out a hard-drivin' blues and throws invisible ingredients into the big, black pot.*)

FIRST YA ADD A PINCH OF STYLE
AND THEN A DASH OF FLAIR
NOW YA STIR IN SOME PREOCCUPATION
WITH THE TEXTURE OF YOUR HAIR

NEXT YA ADD ALL KINDS OF RHYTHMS
LOTS OF FEELINGS AND PIZAZZ
THEN HUNNY THROW IN SOME RAGE
TILL IT CONGEALS AND TURNS TO JAZZ

NOW YOU COOKIN'
COOKIN' WITH AUNT ETHEL
YOU REALLY COOKIN'
COOKIN' WITH AUNT ETHEL, OH YEAH

NOW YA ADD A HEAP OF SURVIVAL
AND HUMILITY, JUST A TOUCH
ADD SOME ATTITUDE
OOPS! I PUT TOO MUCH

AND NOW A WHOLE LOT OF HUMOR
SALTY LANGUAGE, MIXED WITH SADNESS
THEN THROW IN A BOX OF BLUES
AND SIMMER TO MADNESS

NOW YOU COOKIN'
COOKIN' WITH AUNT ETHEL, OH YEAH!

NOW YOU BEAT IT—REALLY WORK IT
DISCARD AND DISOWN
AND IN A FEW HUNDRED YEARS
ONCE IT'S AGED AND FULLY GROWN
YA PUT IT IN THE OVEN
TILL IT'S BLACK
AND HAS A SHEEN
OR TILL IT'S NICE AND YELLA
OR ANY SHADE IN BETWEEN

NEXT YA TAKE 'EM OUT AND COOL 'EM
'CAUSE THEY NO FUN WHEN THEY HOT
AND WON'T YOU BE SURPRISED
AT THE CONCOCTION YOU GOT

YOU HAVE BAKED
BAKED YOURSELF A BATCH OF NEGROES
YES YOU HAVE BAKED YOURSELF
BAKED YOURSELF A BATCH OF NEGROES

(*She pulls from the pot a handful of Negroes, black dolls.*)

But don't ask me what to do with 'em now that you got 'em,
'cause child, that's your problem. (*She throws the dolls back into
the pot.*) But in any case, yaw be sure to join Aunt Ethel next
week, when we gonna be servin' ourselves up some chitlin
quiche . . . some grits-under-glass,

AND A SWEET POTATO PIE
AND YOU'LL BE COOKIN'
COOKIN' WITH AUNT ETHEL
OH YEAH!

(*On* AUNT ETHEL's *final rift, lights reveal . . .*)

The Photo Session

(. . . *a very glamorous, gorgeous, black couple, wearing the best of everything and perfect smiles. The stage is bathed in color and bright white light. Disco music with the chant: "We're fabulous" plays in the background. As they pose, larger-than-life images of their perfection are projected on the museum walls. The music quiets and the images fade away as they begin to speak and pose.*)

GIRL: The world was becoming too much for us.

GUY: We couldn't resolve the contradictions of our existence.

GIRL: And we couldn't resolve yesterday's pain.

GUY: So we gave away our life and we now live inside *Ebony Magazine.*

GIRL: Yes, we live inside a world where everyone is beautiful, and wears fabulous clothes.

GUY: And no one says anything profound.

GIRL: Or meaningful.

GUY: Or contradictory.

GIRL: Because no one talks. Everyone just smiles and shows off their cheekbones.

(*They adopt a profile pose.*)

GUY: Last month I was black and fabulous while holding up a bottle of vodka.

GIRL: This month we get to be black and fabulous together.

(*They dance/pose. The "We're fabulous" chant builds and then fades as they start to speak again.*)

GIRL: There are of course setbacks.

GUY: We have to smile like this for a whole month.

GIRL: And we have no social life.

GUY: And no sex.

GIRL: And at times it feels like we're suffocating, like we're not human anymore.

GUY: And everything is rehearsed, including this other kind of pain we're starting to feel.

GIRL: The kind of pain that comes from feeling no pain at all.

(*They then speak and pose with a sudden burst of energy.*)

GUY: But one can't have everything.

GIRL: Can one?

GUY: So if the world is becoming too much for you, do like we did.

GIRL: Give away your life and come be beautiful with us.

GUY: We guarantee, no contradictions.

GIRL/GUY: Smile/click, smile/click, smile/click.

GIRL: And no pain.

(*They adopt a final pose and revolve off as the "We're fabulous" chant plays and fades into the background.*)

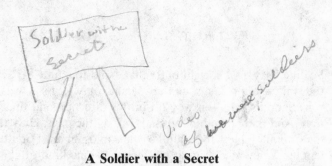

A Soldier with a Secret

(*Projected onto the museum walls are the faces of black soldiers—from the Spanish-American thru to the Vietnam War. Lights slowly reveal* JUNIE ROBINSON, *a black combat soldier, posed on an onyx plinth. He comes to life and smiles at the audience. Somewhat dim-witted, he has an easy-going charm about him.*)

JUNIE: Pst. Pst. Guess what? I know the secret. The secret to your pain. 'Course, I didn't always know. First I had to die, then come back to life, 'fore I had the gift.

Ya see the Cappin sent me off up ahead to scout for screamin' yella bastards. 'Course, for the life of me I couldn't understand why they'd be screamin', seein' as how we was tryin' to kill them and they us.

But anyway, I'm off lookin', when all of a sudden I find myself caught smack dead in the middle of this explosion. This blindin', burnin', scaldin' explosion. Musta been a booby trap or something, 'cause all around me is fire. Hell, I'm on fire. Like a piece of chicken dropped in a skillet of cracklin' grease. Why, my flesh was justa peelin' off of my bones.

But then I says to myself, "Junie, if yo' flesh is on fire, how come you don't feel no pain!" And I didn't. I swear as I'm standin' here, I felt nuthin'. That's when I sort of put two and two together and realized I didn't feel no whole lot of hurtin' cause I done died.

Well I just picked myself up and walked right on out of that explosion. Hell, once you know you dead, why keep on dyin', ya know?

So, like I say, I walk right outta that explosion, fully expectin' to see white clouds, Jesus, and my Mama, only all I saw was more war. Shootin' goin' on way off in this direction and that direction. And there, standin' around, was all the guys. Hubert, J.F., the Cappin. I guess the sound of the explosion must of attracted 'em, and they all starin' at me like I'm some kind of ghost.

So I yells to 'em, "Hey there Hubert! Hey there Cappin!" But they just stare. So I tells 'em how I'd died and how I guess it wasn't my time 'cause here I am, "Fully in the flesh and not a scratch to my bones." And they still just stare. So I took to starin' back.

(*The expression on* JUNIE'*s face slowly turns to horror and disbelief.*)

Only what I saw . . . well I can't exactly to this day describe it. But I swear, as sure as they was wearin' green and holdin' guns, they was each wearin' a piece of the future on their faces.

Yeah. All the hurt that was gonna get done to them and they was gonna do to folks was right there clear as day.

I saw how J.F., once he got back to Chicago, was gonna get shot dead by this po-lice, and I saw how Hubert was gonna start beatin' up on his old lady which I didn't understand, 'cause all he could do was talk on and on about how much he loved her. Each and every one of 'em had pain in his future and blood on his path. And God or the Devil one spoke to me and said, "Junie, these colored boys ain't gonna be the same after this war. They ain't gonna have no kind of happiness."

Well right then and there it come to me. The secret to their pain.

Late that night, after the medics done checked me over and found me fit for fightin', after everybody done settle down for the night, I sneaked over to where Hubert was sleepin', and with a needle I stole from the medics . . . pst, pst . . . I shot a little air into his veins. The second he died, all the hurtin-to-come just left his face.

Two weeks later I got J.F. and after that Woodrow . . . Jimmy Joe . . . I even spent all night waitin' by the latrine 'cause I knew the Cappin always made a late night visit and pst . . . pst . . . I got him.

(*Smiling, quite proud of himself.*) That's how come I died and come back to life. 'Cause just like Jesus went around healin' the sick, I'm supposed to go around healin' the hurtin' all these colored boys wearin' from the war.

Pst, pst. I know the secret. The secret to your pain. The secret to yours, and yours. Pst. Pst. Pst. Pst.

(*The lights slowly fade.*)

The Gospel According to Miss Roj

(*The darkness is cut by electronic music. Cold, pounding, unrelenting. A neon sign which spells out THE BOTTOMLESS PIT clicks on. There is a lone bar stool. Lights flash on and off, pulsating to the beat. There is a blast of smoke and, from the haze,* MISS ROJ *appears. He is dressed in striped patio pants, white go-go boots, a halter, and cat-shaped sunglasses. What would seem ridiculous on anyone else,* MISS ROJ *wears as if it were high fashion. He carries himself with total elegance and absolute arrogance.*)

MISS ROJ: God created black people and black people created style. The name's Miss Roj . . . that's R.O.J. thank you and you can find me every Wednesday, Friday and Saturday nights at "The Bottomless Pit," the watering hole for the wild and weary which asks the question, "Is there life after Jherri-curl?"

(*A waiter enters, hands* MISS ROJ *a drink, and then exits.*)

Thanks, doll. *Yes,* if they be black and swish, the B.P. has seen them, which is not to suggest the Pit is lacking in cultural diversity. Oh no. There are your dinge queens, white men who like their chicken legs dark. (*He winks/flirts with a man in the audience.*) And let's not forget, "Los Muchachos de la Neighborhood." But the speciality of the house is The Snap Queens. (*He snaps his fingers.*) We are a rare breed.

For, you see, when something strikes our fancy, when the truth comes piercing through the dark, well you just can't let it pass unnoticed. No darling. You must pronounce it with a snap. (*He snaps.*)

Snapping comes from another galaxy, as do all snap queens. That's right. I ain't just your regular oppressed American Negro. No-no-no! I am an extraterrestial. And I ain't talkin' none of that shit you seen in the movies! I have real power.

(*The waiter enters.* MISS ROJ *stops him.*)

Speaking of no power, will you please tell Miss Stingy-with-the-rum, that if Miss Roj had wanted to remain sober, she could have stayed home and drank Kool-aid. (*He snaps.*) Thank you.

(*The waiter exits.* MISS ROJ *crosses and sits on bar stool.*)

Yes, I was placed here on Earth to study the life habits of a deteriorating society, and child when we talkin' New York City, we are discussing the Queen of Deterioration. Miss New York is doing a slow dance with death, and I am here to warn you all, but before I do, I must know . . . don't you just love my patio pants? Annette Funicello immortalized them in "Beach Blanket Bingo," and I have continued the legacy. And my go-gos? I realize white after Labor Day is very gauche, but as the saying goes, if you've got it flaunt it, if you don't, front it and snap to death any bastard who dares to defy you. (*Laughing*) Oh ho! My demons are showing. Yes, my demons live at the bottom of my Bacardi and Coke.

Let's just hope for all concerned I dance my demons out before I drink them out 'cause child, dancing demons take you on a ride, but those drinkin' demons just take you, and you find yourself doing the strangest things. Like the time I locked my father in the broom closet. Seems the liquor made his tongue real liberal and he decided he was gonna baptize me with the word "faggot" over and over. Well, he's just going on and on with "faggot this" and "faggot that," all the while walking toward the broom closet to piss. So the demons just took hold of my wedges and forced me to kick the drunk son-of-a-bitch into the closet and lock the door. (*Laughter*) Three days later I remembered he was there. (*He snaps.*)

(*The waiter enters.* MISS ROJ *takes a drink and downs it.*)

Another!

(*The waiter exits.*)

(*Dancing about.*) Oh yes-yes-yes! Miss Roj is quintessential style. I corn row the hairs on my legs so that they spell out M.I.S.S. R.O.J. And I dare any bastard to fuck with me because I will snap your ass into oblivion.

I have the power, you know. Everytime I snap, I steal one beat of your heart. So if you find yourself gasping for air in the middle of the night, chances are you fucked with Miss Roj and she didn't like it.

Like the time this asshole at Jones Beach decided to take issue with my coulotte-sailor ensemble. This child, this muscle-bound Brooklyn thug in a skin-tight bikini, very skin-tight so the whole world can see that instead of a brain, God gave him an extra thick piece of sausage. You know the kind who beat up on their wives for breakfast. Snap your fingers if you know what I'm talking about . . . Come on and snap, child. (*He gets the audience to snap.*) Well, he decided to blurt out when I walked by, "Hey look at da monkey coon in da faggit suit." Well, I walked up to the poor dear, very calmly lifted my hand, and. . . . (*He snaps in rapid succession.*) A heart attack, right there on the beach. (*He singles out someone in the audience.*) You don't believe it? Cross me! Come on! Come on!

(*The waiter enters, hands* MISS ROJ *a drink.* MISS ROJ *downs it. The waiter exits.*)

(*Looking around.*) If this place is the answer, we're asking all the wrong questions. The only reason I come here is to communicate with my origins. The flashing lights are signals from my planet way out there. Yes, girl, even further than Flatbush. We're talking another galaxy. The flashing lights tell me how much time is left before the end.

(*Very drunk and loud by now.*) I hate the people here. I hate the drinks. But most of all I hate this goddamn music. That ain't music. Give me Aretha Franklin any day. (*Singing*) "Just a little respect. R.E.S.P.E.C.T." Yeah! Yeah!

Come on and dance your last dance with Miss Roj. Last call is but a drink away and each snap puts you one step closer to the end.

A high-rise goes up. You can't get no job. Come on everybody and dance. A whole race of people gets trashed and debased. Snap those fingers and dance. Some sick bitch throws her baby out the window 'cause she thinks it's the Devil. Everybody snap! *The New York Post.* Snap!

Snap for every time you walk past someone lying in the street, smelling like frozen piss and shit and you don't see it. Snap for every crazed bastard who kills himself so as to get the jump on being killed. And snap for every sick muthafucker who, bored with carrying around his fear, takes to shooting up other people.

Yeah, snap your fingers and dance with Miss Roj. But don't be fooled by the banners and balloons 'cause, child, this ain't no party going on. Hell no! It's a wake. And the casket's made out of stone, steel, and glass and the people are racing all over the pavement like maggots on a dead piece of meat.

Yeah, dance! But don't be surprised if there ain't no beat holding you together 'cause we traded in our drums for respectability. So now it's just words. Words rappin'. Words screechin'. Words flowin' instead of blood 'cause you know that don't work. Words cracklin' instead of fire 'cause by the time a match is struck on 125th Street and you run to midtown, the flame has been blown away.

So come on and dance with Miss Roj and her demons. We don't ask for acceptance. We don't ask for approval. We know who we are and we move on it!

I guarantee you will never hear two fingers put together in a snap and not think of Miss Roj. That's power, baby. Patio pants and all.

(*The lights begin to flash in rapid succession.*)

So let's dance! And snap! And dance! And snap!

(MISS ROJ *begins to dance as if driven by his demons. There is a blast of smoke and when the haze settles,* MISS ROJ *has revolved off and in place of him is a recording of Aretha Franklin singing "Respect.")*

The Hairpiece

(*As "Respect" fades into the background, a vanity revolves to center stage. On this vanity are two wigs, an Afro wig, circa 1968, and a long, flowing wig, both resting on wig stands. A black* WOMAN *enters, her head and body wrapped in towels. She picks up a framed picture and after a few moments of hesitation, throws it into a small trash can. She then removes one of her towels to reveal a totally bald head. Looking into a mirror on the "fourth wall," she begins applying makeup.*)

(*The wig stand holding the Afro wig opens her eyes. Her name is* JANINE. *She stares in disbelief at the bald woman.*)

JANINE: (*Calling to the other wig stand.*) LaWanda. LaWanda girl, wake up.

(*The other wig stand, the one with the long, flowing wig, opens her eyes. Her name is* LAWANDA.)

LAWANDA: What? What is it?

JANINE: Check out girlfriend.

LAWANDA: Oh, girl, I don't believe it.

JANINE: (*Laughing*) Just look at the poor thing, trying to paint some life onto that face of hers. You'd think by now she'd realize it's the hair. It's all about the hair.

LAWANDA: What hair! She ain't got no hair! She done fried, dyed, de-chemicalized her shit to death.

JANINE: And all that's left is that buck-naked scalp of hers, sittin' up there apologizin' for being odd-shaped and ugly.

LAWANDA: (*Laughing with* JANINE.) Girl, stop!

JANINE: I ain't sayin' nuthin' but the truth.

LAWANDA/JANINE: The bitch is bald! (*They laugh.*)

JANINE: And all over some man.

LAWANDA: I tell ya, girl, I just don't understand it. I mean, look at her. She's got a right nice face, a good head on her shoulders. A good job even. And she's got to go fall in love with that fool.

JANINE: That political quick-change artist. Everytime the nigga went and changed his ideology, she went and changed her hair to fit the occasion.

LAWANDA: Well at least she's breaking up with him.

JANINE: Hunny, no!

LAWANDA: Yes child.

JANINE: Oh, girl, dish me the dirt!

LAWANDA: Well, you see, I heard her on the phone, talking to one of her girlfriends, and she's meeting him for lunch today to give him the ax.

JANINE: Well it's about time.

LAWANDA: I hear ya. But don't you worry 'bout a thing, girlfriend. I'm gonna tell you all about it.

JANINE: Hunny, you won't have to tell me a damn thing 'cause I'm gonna be there, front row, center.

LAWANDA: You?

JANINE: Yes, child, she's wearing me to lunch.

LAWANDA: (*Outraged*) I don't think so!

JANINE: (*With an attitude*) What do you mean, you don't think so?

LAWANDA: Exactly what I said, "I don't think so." Damn, Janine, get real. How the hell she gonna wear both of us?

JANINE: She ain't wearing both of us. She's wearing me.

LAWANDA: Says who?

JANINE: Says me! Says her! Ain't that right, girlfriend?

(*The* WOMAN *stops putting on makeup, looks around, sees no one, and goes back to her makeup.*)

JANINE: I said, ain't that right!

(*The* WOMAN *picks up the phone.*)

WOMAN: Hello . . . hello . . .

JANINE: Did you hear the damn phone ring?

WOMAN: No.

JANINE: Then put the damn phone down and talk to me.

WOMAN: I ah . . . don't understand.

JANINE: It ain't deep so don't panic. Now, you're having lunch with your boyfriend, right?

WOMAN: (*Breaking into tears.*) I think I'm having a nervous breakdown.

JANINE: (*Impatient*) I said you're having lunch with your boyfriend, right!

WOMAN: (*Scared, pulling herself together.*) Yes, right . . . right.

JANINE: To break up with him.

WOMAN: How did you know that?

LAWANDA: I told her.

WOMAN: (*Stands and screams.*) Help! Help!

JANINE: Sit down. I said sit your ass down!

(*The* WOMAN *does.*)

JANINE: Now set her straight and tell her you're wearing me.

LAWANDA: She's the one that needs to be set straight, so go on and tell her you're wearing me.

JANINE: No, tell her you're wearing me.

(*There is a pause.*)

LAWANDA: Well?

JANINE: Well?

WOMAN: I ah . . . actually hadn't made up my mind.

JANINE: (*Going off*) What do you mean you ain't made up you mind! After all that fool has put you through, you gonna need all the attitude you can get and there is nothing like attitude and a healthy head of kinks to make his shit shrivel like it should!

That's right! When you wearin' me, you lettin' him know he ain't gonna get no sweet-talkin' comb through your love without some serious resistance. No-no! The kink of my head is like the kink of your heart and neither is about to be hot-pressed into surrender.

LAWANDA: That shit is so tired. The last time attitude worked on anybody was 1968. Janine girl, you need to get over it and get on with it. (*To the* WOMAN.) And you need to give the nigga a goodbye he will never forget.

I say give him hysteria! Give him emotion! Give him rage! And there is nothing like a toss of the tresses to make your emotional outburst shine with emotional flair.

You can toss me back, shake me from side to side, all the while screaming, "I want you out of my life forever!!!" And not only will I come bouncing back for more, but you just might win an Academy Award for best performance by a head of hair in a dramatic role.

JANINE: Miss hunny, please! She don't need no Barbie doll dipped in chocolate telling her what to do. She needs a head of hair that's coming from a fo' real place.

LAWANDA: Don't you dare talk about nobody coming from a "fo' real place," Miss Made-in-Taiwan!

JANINE: Hey! I ain't ashamed of where I come from. Besides, it don't matter where you come from as long as you end up in the right place.

LAWANDA: And it don't matter the grade as long as the point gets made. So go on and tell her you're wearing me.

JANINE: No, tell her you're wearing me.

(*The* WOMAN, *unable to take it, begins to bite off her fake nails, as* LAWANDA *and* JANINE *go at each other.*)

LAWANDA:
Set the bitch straight. Let her know there is no way she could even begin to compete with me. I am quality. She is kink. I am exotic. She is common. I am class and she is trash. That's

JANINE:
Who you callin' a bitch? Why, if I had hands I'd knock you clear into next week. You think you cute. She thinks she's cute just 'cause that synthetic mop of hers blows in the wind. She

right. T.R.A.S.H. We're talking three strikes and you're out. So go on and tell her you're wearing me. Go on, tell her! Tell her! Tell her! looks like a fool and you look like an even bigger fool when you wear her, so go on and tell her you're wearing me. Go on, tell her! Tell her! Tell her!

(*The* WOMAN *screams and pulls the two wigs off the wig stands as the lights go to black on three bald heads.*)

The Last Mama-on-the-Couch Play

(*A* NARRATOR, *dressed in a black tuxedo, enters through the audience and stands center stage. He is totally solemn.*)

NARRATOR: We are pleased to bring you yet another Mama-on-the-Couch play. A searing domestic drama that tears at the very fabric of racist America. (*He crosses upstage center and sits on a stool and reads from a playscript.*) Act One. Scene One.

(MAMA *revolves on stage left, sitting on a couch reading a large, oversized Bible. A window is placed stage right.* MAMA's *dress, the couch, and drapes are made from the same material. A doormat lays down center.*)

NARRATOR: Lights up on a dreary, depressing, but with middle-class aspirations tenement slum. There is a couch, with a Mama on it. Both are well worn. There is a picture of Jesus on the wall . . . (*A picture of Jesus is instantly revealed.*) . . . and a window which looks onto an abandoned tenement. It is late spring.

Enter Walter-Lee-Beau-Willie-Jones (SON *enters through the audience.*) He is Mama's thirty-year-old son. His brow is heavy from three hundred years of oppression.

MAMA: (*Looking up from her Bible, speaking in a slow manner.*) Son, did you wipe your feet?

SON: (*An ever-erupting volcano.*) No, Mama, I didn't wipe me feet! Out there, every day, Mama is the Man. The Man Mama. Mr. Charlie! Mr. Bossman! And he's wipin' his feet on me. On me, Mama, every damn day of my life. Ain't that enough for me to deal with? Ain't that enough?

MAMA: Son, wipe your feet.

SON: I wanna dream. I wanna be somebody. I wanna take charge of my life.

MAMA: You can do all of that, but first you got to wipe your feet.

SON: (*As he crosses to the mat, mumbling and wiping his feet.*) Wipe my feet . . . wipe my feet . . . wipe my feet . . .

MAMA: That's a good boy.

SON: (*Exploding*) Boy! Boy! I don't wanna be nobody's good boy, Mama. I wanna be my own man!

MAMA: I know son, I know. God will show the way.

SON: God, Mama! Since when did your God ever do a damn thing for the black man. Huh, Mama, huh? You tell me. When did your God ever help me?

MAMA: (*Removing her wire-rim glasses.*) Son, come here.

(SON *crosses to* MAMA, *who slowly stands and in a exaggerated stage slap, backhands* SON *clear across the stage. The* NARRATOR *claps his hands to create the sound for the slap.* MAMA *then lifts her clinched fists to the heavens.*)

MAMA: Not in my house, my house, will you ever talk that way again!

(*The* NARRATOR, *so moved by her performance, erupts in applause and encourages the audience to do so.*)

NARRATOR: Beautiful. Just stunning.

(*He reaches into one of the secret compartments of the set and gets an award which he ceremoniously gives to* MAMA *for her performance. She bows and then returns to the couch.*)

NARRATOR: Enter Walter-Lee-Beau-Willie's wife, The Lady in Plaid.

(*Music from nowhere is heard, a jazzy pseudo-abstract intro as the*
LADY IN PLAID *dances in through the audience, wipes her feet, and
then twirls about.*)

LADY:
   She was a creature of regal beauty
   who in ancient time graced the temples of the Nile
   with her womanliness
   But here she was, stuck being colored
   and a woman in a world that valued neither.

SON: You cooked my dinner?

LADY: (*Oblivious to* SON.)
   Feet flat, back broke,
   she looked at the man who, though he be thirty,
   still ain't got his own apartment.
   Yeah, he's still livin' with his Mama!
   And she asked herself, was this the life
   for a Princess Colored, who by the
   translucence of her skin, knew the
   universe was her sister.

(*The* LADY IN PLAID *twirls and dances.*)

SON: (*Becoming irate.*) I've had a hard day of dealin' with the Man.
   Where's my damn dinner? Woman, stand still when I'm talkin'
   to you!

LADY: And she cried for her sisters in Detroit
   Who knew, as she, that their souls belonged
   in ancient temples on the Nile.
   And she cried for her sisters in Chicago
   who, like her, their life has become
   one colored hell.

SON: There's only one thing gonna get through to you.

LADY: And she cried for her sisters in New Orleans
   And her sisters in Trenton and Birmingham,
   and

Poughkeepsie and Orlando and Miami Beach
and
Las Vegas, Palm Springs.

(*As she continues to call out cities, he crosses offstage and returns with two black dolls and then crosses to the window.*)

SON: Now are you gonna cook me dinner?

LADY: Walter-Lee-Beau-Willie-Jones, no! Not my babies.

(SON *throws them out the window. The* LADY IN PLAID *then lets out a primal scream.*)

LADY: He dropped them!!!!

(*The* NARRATOR *breaks into applause.*)

NARRATOR: Just splendid. Shattering.

(*He then crosses and after an intense struggle with* MAMA, *he takes the award from her and gives it to the* LADY IN PLAID, *who is still suffering primal pain.*)

LADY: Not my babies . . . not my . . . (*Upon receiving the award, she instantly recovers.*) Help me up, sugar. (*She then bows and crosses and stands behind the couch.*)

NARRATOR: Enter Medea Jones, Walter-Lee-Beau-Willie's sister.

(MEDEA *moves very ceremoniously, wiping her feet and then speaking and gesturing as if she just escaped from a Greek tragedy.*)

MEDEA:
Ah, see how the sun kneels to speak
her evening vespers, exaulting all
in her vision, even lowly tenement
long abandoned.

Mother, wife of brother, I trust
the approaching darkness finds you
safe in Hestia's busom.

Brother, why wear the face of a man
in anguish. Can the garment of thine
feelings cause the shape of your
countenance to disfigure so?

SON: (*At the end of his rope.*) Leave me alone, Medea.

MEDEA: (*To* MAMA)
Is good brother still going on and on and on
about He and The Man.

MAMA/LADY: What else?

MEDEA: Ah brother, if with our thoughts and
words we could cast thine oppressors
into the lowest bowels of wretched
hell, would that make us more like the
gods or more like our oppressors.

No, brother, no, do not let thy rage
choke the blood which anoints thy
heart with love. Forgo thine darkened
humor and let love shine on your
soul, like a jewel on a young maiden's hand.

(*Dropping to her knees.*)

I beseech thee, forgo thine
anger and leave wrath to the gods!

SON: Girl, what has gotten into you.

MEDEA: Juilliard, good brother. For I am no
longer bound by rhythms of race or
region. Oh, no. My speech, like my
pain and suffering, have become
classical and therefore universal.

LADY: I didn't understand a damn thing she said, but girl you usin'
them words.

(LADY IN PLAID *crosses and gives* MEDEA *the award and everyone applauds.*)

SON: (*Trying to stop the applause.*) Wait one damn minute! This my play. It's about me and the Man. It ain't got nuthin' to do with no ancient temples on the Nile and it ain't got nuthin' to do with Hestia's busom. And it ain't got nuthin' to do with you slappin' me across no room. (*His gut-wrenching best.*) It's about me. Me and my pain! My pain!

THE VOICE OF THE MAN: Walter-Lee-Beau-Willie, this is the Man. You have been convicted of overacting. Come out with your hands up.

(SON *starts to cross to the window.*)

SON: Well now that does it.

MAMA: Son, no, don't go near that window. Son, no!

(*Gun shots ring out and* SON *falls dead.*)

MAMA: (*Crossing to the body, too emotional for words.*) My son, he was a good boy. Confused. Angry. Just like his father. And his father's father. And his father's father's father. And now he's dead.

(*Seeing she's about to drop to her knees, the* NARRATOR *rushes and places a pillow underneath her just in time.*)

If only he had been born into a world better than this. A world where there are no well-worn couches and no well-worn Mamas and nobody overemotes.

If only he had been born into an all-black musical.

(*A song intro begins.*)

Nobody ever dies in an all-black musical.

(MEDEA *and* LADY IN PLAID *pull out church fans and begin to fan themselves.*)

MAMA: (*Singing a soul-stirring gospel.*)
OH WHY COULDN'T HE
BE BORN
INTO A SHOW WITH LOTS OF SINGING
AND DANCING

I SAY WHY
COULDN'T HE
BE BORN

LADY: Go ahead hunny. Take your time.

MAMA:
INTO A SHOW WHERE EVERYBODY
IS HAPPY

NARRATOR/MEDEA: Preach! Preach!

MAMA:
OH WHY COULDN'T HE BE BORN WITH THE
    CHANCE
TO SMILE A LOT AND SING AND DANCE
OH WHY
OH WHY

OH WHY
COULDN'T HE
BE BORN
INTO AN ALL-BLACK SHOW
WOAH-WOAH

(*The* CAST *joins in, singing do-wop gospel background to* MAMA'*s lament.*)

OH WHY
COULDN'T HE
BE BORN
(HE BE BORN)

INTO A SHOW WHERE EVERYBODY
IS HAPPY

WHY COULDN'T HE BE BORN WITH THE
    CHANCE
TO SMILE A LOT AND SING AND DANCE
WANNA KNOW WHY
WANNA KNOW WHY

OH WHY
COULDN'T HE
BE BORN
INTO ALL ALL-BLACK SHOW
A-MEN

(*A singing/dancing, spirit-raising revival begins.*)

OH, SON, GET UP
GET UP AND DANCE
WE SAY GET UP
THIS IS YOUR SECOND CHANCE

DON'T SHAKE A FIST
JUST SHAKE A LEG
AND DO THE TWIST
DON'T SCREAM AND BEG
SON SON SON
GET UP AND DANCE

GET
GET UP
GET UP AND
GET UP AND DANCE—ALL RIGHT!
GET UP AND DANCE—ALL RIGHT!
GET UP AND DANCE!

(WALTER-LEE-BEAU-WILLIE *springs to life and joins in the dancing. A
foot-stomping, hand-clapping production number takes off, which
encompasses a myriad of black-Broadwayesque dancing styles—
shifting speeds and styles with exuberant abandonment.*)

MAMA: (*Bluesy*)
   WHY COULDN'T HE BE BORN INTO AN ALL-BLACK
   SHOW

CAST:
   WITH SINGING AND DANCING

MAMA: BLACK SHOW

(MAMA *scats and the dancing becomes manic and just a little too desperate to please.*)

CAST:
   WE GOTTA DANCE
   WE GOTTA DANCE
   GET UP GET UP GET UP AND DANCE
   WE GOTTA DANCE
   WE GOTTA DANCE
   GOTTA DANCE!

(*Just at the point the dancing is about to become violent, the cast freezes and pointedly, simply sings:*)

   IF WE WANT TO LIVE
   WE HAVE GOT TO
   WE HAVE GOT TO
   DANCE . . . AND DANCE . . . AND DANCE . . .

(*As they continue to dance with zombie-like frozen smiles and faces, around them images of coon performers flash as the lights slowly fade.*)

Symbiosis

(*The Temptations singing "My Girl" are heard as lights reveal a* BLACK MAN *in corporate dress standing before a large trash can throwing objects from a Saks Fifth Avenue bag into it. Circling around him with his every emotion on his face is* THE KID, *who is dressed in a late-sixties street style. His moves are slightly heightened. As the scene begins the music fades.*)

MAN: (*With contained emotions.*)
 My first pair of Converse All-stars. Gone.
 My first Afro-comb. Gone.
 My first dashiki. Gone.
 My autographed pictures of Stokley Carmichael, Jomo Kenyatta and Donna Summer. Gone.

KID: (*Near tears, totally upset.*) This shit's not fair man. Damn! Hell! Shit! Shit! It's not fair!

MAN:
 My first jar of Murray's Pomade.
 My first can of Afro-sheen.
 My first box of curl relaxer. Gone! Gone! Gone!
 Eldridge Cleaver's *Soul on Ice.*

KID: Not *Soul on Ice!*

MAN: It's been replaced on my bookshelf by *The Color Purple.*

KID: (*Horrified*) No!

MAN: Gone!

KID: But—

MAN:
Jimi Hendrix's "Purple Haze." Gone.
Sly Stone's "There's A Riot Goin' On." Gone.
The Jackson Five's "I Want You Back."

KID: Man, you can't throw that away. It's living proof Michael had a black nose.

MAN: It's all going. Anything and everything that connects me to you, to who I was, to what we were, is out of my life.

KID: You've got to give me another chance.

MAN: *Fingertips Part 2.*

KID: Man, how can you do that? That's vintage Stevie Wonder.

MAN: You want to know how, Kid? You want to know how? Because my survival depends on it. Whether you know it or not, the Ice Age is upon us.

KID: (*Jokingly*) Man, what the hell you talkin' about. It's 95 damn degrees.

MAN: The climate is changing, Kid, and either you adjust or you end up extinct. A sociological dinosaur. Do you understand what I'm trying to tell you? King Kong would have made it to the top if only he had taken the elevator. Instead he brought attention to his struggle and ended up dead.

KID: (*Pleading*) I'll change. I swear I'll change. I'll maintain a low profile. You won't even know I'm around.

MAN: If I'm to become what I'm to become then you've got to go. . . . I have no history. I have no past.

KID: Just like that?

MAN: (*Throwing away a series of buttons.*) Free Angela! Free Bobby! Free Huey, Duey, and Louie! U.S. out of Viet Nam.

U.S. out of Cambodia. U.S. out of Harlem, Detroit, and New-
ark. Gone! . . . The Temptations Greatest Hits!

KID: (*Grabbing the album.*) No!!!

MAN: Give it back, Kid.

KID: No.

MAN: I said give it back!

KID: No. I can't let you trash this. Johnny man, it contains fourteen
classic cuts by the tempting Temptations. We're talking, "Ain't
Too Proud to Beg," "Papa Was a Rolling Stone," "My Girl."

MAN: (*Warning*) I don't have all day.

KID: For God's sake, Johnny man, "My Girl" is the jam to end all
jams. It's what we are. Who we are. It's a way of life. Come on,
man, for old times sake. (*Singing*)

I GOT SUNSHINE ON A CLOUDY DAY
BUM-DA-DUM-DA-DUM-DA-BUM
AND WHEN IT'S COLD OUTSIDE

Come on, Johnny man, you ain't "bummin'," man.

I GOT THE MONTH OF MAY

Here comes your favorite part. Come on, Johnny man, sing.

I GUESS YOU SAY
WHAT CAN MAKE ME FEEL THIS WAY
MY GIRL, MY GIRL, MY GIRL
TALKIN' 'BOUT

MAN: (*Exploding*) I said give it back!

KID: (*Angry*) I ain't givin' you a muthafuckin' thing!

MAN: Now you listen to me!

KID: No, you listen to me. This is the Kid you're dealin' with, so don't fuck with me!

(*He hits his fist into his hand, and* THE MAN *grabs for his heart.* THE KID *repeats with two more hits, which causes the man to drop to the ground, grabbing his heart.*)

KID: Jai! Jai! Jai!

MAN: Kid, please.

KID: Yeah. Yeah. Now who's begging who. . . . Well, well, well, look at Mr. Cream-of-the-Crop, Mr. Colored-Man-on-Top. Now that he's making it, he no longer wants anything to do with the Kid. Well, you may put all kinds of silk ties 'round your neck and white lines up your nose, but the Kid is here to stay. You may change your women as often as you change your underwear, but the Kid is here to stay. And regardless of how much of your past that you trash, I ain't goin' no damn where. Is that clear? Is that clear?

MAN: (*Regaining his strength, beginning to stand.*) Yeah.

KID: Good. (*After a beat.*) You all right man? You all right? I don't want to hurt you, but when you start all that talk about getting rid of me, well, it gets me kind of crazy. We need each other. We are one . . .

(*Before* THE KID *can complete his sentence,* THE MAN *grabs him around his neck and starts to choke him violently.*)

MAN: (*As he strangles him.*) The . . . Ice . . . Age . . . is . . . upon us . . . and either we adjust . . . or we end up . . . extinct.

(THE KID *hangs limp in* THE MAN'*s arms.*)

MAN: (*Laughing*) Man kills his own rage. Film at eleven. (*He then dumps* THE KID *into the trash can, and closes the lid. He speaks in a contained voice.*) I have no history. I have no past. I can't. It's too much. It's much too much. I must be able to smile on cue.

And watch the news with an impersonal eye. I have no stake in the madness.

Being black is too emotionally taxing; therefore I will be black only on weekends and holidays.

(*He then turns to go, but sees the Temptations album lying on the ground. He picks it up and sings quietly to himself.*)

I GUESS YOU SAY
WHAT CAN MAKE ME FEEL THIS WAY

(*He pauses, but then crosses to the trash can, lifts the lid, and just as he is about to toss the album in, a hand reaches from inside the can and grabs hold of* THE MAN'*s arm.* THE KID *then emerges from the can with a death grip on* THE MAN'*s arm.*)

KID: (*Smiling*) What's happenin'?

BLACKOUT

Lala's Opening

(*Roving follow spots. A timpani drum roll. As we hear the voice of the* ANNOUNCER, *outrageously glamorous images of* LALA *are projected onto the museum walls.*)

VOICE OF ANNOUNCER: From Rome to Rangoon! Paris to Prague! We are pleased to present the American debut of the one! The only! The breathtaking! The astounding! The stupendous! The incredible! The magnificent! Lala Lamazing Grace!

(*Thunderous applause as* LALA *struts on, the definitive black diva. She has long, flowing hair, an outrageous lamé dress, and an affected French accent which she loses when she's upset.*)

LALA:
EVERYBODY LOVES LALA
EVERYBODY LOVES ME
PARIS! BERLIN! LONDON! ROME!
NO MATTER WHERE I GO
I ALWAYS FEEL AT HOME

OHHHH
EVERYBODY LOVES LALA
EVERYBODY LOVES ME
I'M TRES MAGNIFIQUE
AND OH SO UNIQUE
AND WHEN IT COMES TO GLAMOUR
I'M CHIC-ER THAN CHIC

(*She giggles.*)

THAT'S WHY EVERYBODY
EVERYBODY
EVERYBODY-EVERYBODY-EVERYBODY
LOVES ME

(*She begins to vocally reach for higher and higher notes, until she has to point to her final note. She ends the number with a grand flourish and bows to thunderous applause.*)

LALA: Yes, it's me! Lala Lamazing Grace and I have come home. Home to the home I never knew as home. Home to you, my people, my blood, my guts.

My story is a simple one, full of fire, passion, magique. You may ask how did I, a humble girl from the backwoods of Mississippi, come to be the ninth wonder of the modern world. Well, I can't take all of the credit. Part of it goes to him. (*She points toward the heavens.*)

No, not the light man, darling, but God. For, you see, Lala is a star. A very big star. Let us not mince words, I'm a fucking meteorite. (*She laughs.*) But He is the universe and just like my sister, Aretha la Franklin, Lala's roots are in the black church. (*She sings in a showy gospel style:*)

THAT'S WHY EVERYBODY LOVES
SWING LOW SWEET CHARIOT
THAT'S WHY EVERYBODY LOVES
GO DOWN MOSES WAY DOWN IN EGYPT LAND
THAT'S WHY EVERYBODY EVERYBODY LOVES
ME!!!

(*Once again she points to her final note and then basks in applause.*)

I love that note. I just can't hit it.

Now, before I dazzle you with more of my limitless talent, tell me something, America. (*Musical underscoring*) Why has it taken you so long to recognize my artistry? Mother France opened her loving arms and Lala came running. All over the world Lala was embraced. But here, ha! You spat at Lala. Was I too exotic? Too much woman, or what?

Diana Ross you embrace. A two-bit nobody from Detroit, of all places. Now, I'm not knocking la Ross. She does the best she

can with the little she has. (*She laughs.*) But the Paul la
Robesons, the James la Baldwins, the Josephine la Baker's, who
was my godmother you know. The Lala Lamazing Grace's you
kick out. You drive . . .

AWAY
I AM GOING AWAY
HOPING TO FIND A BETTER DAY
WHAT DO YOU SAY
HEY HEY
I AM GOING AWAY
AWAY

(LALA, *caught up in the drama of the song, doesn't see* ADMONIA, *her
maid, stick her head out from offstage.*)

(*Once she is sure* LALA *isn't looking, she wheels onto stage right*
FLO'RANCE, LALA'*s lover, who wears a white mask/blonde hair. He is
gagged and tied to a chair.* ADMONIA *places him on stage and then
quickly exits.*)

LALA:
AU REVOIR—JE VAIS PARTIR MAINTENANT
JE VEUX DIRE MAINTENANT
AU REVOIR
AU REVOIR
AU REVOIR
AU REVOIR
A-MA-VIE

(*On her last note, she sees* FLO'RANCE *and, in total shock, crosses to
him.*)

LALA: Flo'rance, what the hell are you doing out here, looking like
that. I haven't seen you for three days and you decide to show
up now?

(*He mumbles.*)

I don't want to hear it!

(*He mumbles.*)

I said shut up!

(ADMONIA *enters from stage right and has a letter opener on a silver tray.*)

ADMONIA: Pst!

(LALA, *embarrassed by the presence of* ADMONIA *on stage, smiles apologetically at the audience.*)

LALA: Un momento.

(*She then pulls* ADMONIA *to the side.*)

LALA: Darling, have you lost your mind coming onstage while I'm performing. And what have you done to Flo'rance? When I asked you to keep him tied up, I didn't mean to tie him up.

(ADMONIA *gives her the letter opener.*)

LALA: Why are you giving me this? I have no letters to open. I'm in the middle of my American debut. Admonia, take Flo'rance off this stage with you! Admonia!

(ADMONIA *is gone.* LALA *turns to the audience and tries to make the best of it.*)

LALA: That was Admonia, my slightly overweight black maid, and this is Flo'rance, my amour. I remember how we met, don't you Flo'rance. I was sitting in a café on the Left Bank, when I looked up and saw the most beautiful man staring down at me.

"Who are you," he asked. I told him my name . . . whatever my name was back then. And he said, "No, that cannot be your name. Your name should fly, like Lala." And the rest is la history.

Flo'rance molded me into the woman I am today. He is my Svengali, my reality, my all. And I thought I was all to him, until we came here to America, and he fucked that bitch. Yeah, you fucked 'em all. Anything black and breathing. And all this time, I thought you loved me for being me. (*She holds the letter opener to his neck.*)

You may think you made me, but I'll have you know I was who I was, whoever that was, long before you made me what I am. So there! (*She stabs him and breaks into song.*)

OH, LOVE CAN DRIVE A WOMAN TO MADNESS
TO PAIN AND SADNESS
I KNOW
BELIEVE ME I KNOW
I KNOW
I KNOW

(LALA *sees what she's done and is about to scream but catches herself and tries to play it off.*)

LALA: Moving right along.

(ADMONIA *enters with a telegram on a tray.*)

ADMONIA: Pst.

LALA: (*Anxious/hostile*) What is it now?

(ADMONIA *hands* LALA *a telegram.*)

LALA: (*Excited*) Oh, la telegram from one of my fans and the concert isn't even over yet. Get me the letter opener. It's in Flo'rance.

(ADMONIA *hands* LALA *the letter opener.*)

LALA: Next I am going to do for you my immortal hit song, "The Girl Inside." But first we open the telegram. (*She quickly reads it and is outraged.*) What! Which pig in la audience wrote this trash? (*Reading*) "Dear Sadie, I'm so proud. The show's wonderful, but talk less and sing more. Love, Mama."

First off, no one calls me Sadie. Sadie died the day Lala was born. And secondly, my Mama's dead. Anyone who knows anything about Lala Lamazing Grace knows that my mother and Josephine Baker were French patriots together. They infiltrated a carnival rumored to be the center of Nazi intelligence, disguised as Hottentot Siamese twins. You may laugh but it's true. Mama died a heroine. It's all in my autobiography, "Voilá Lala!" So whoever sent this telegram is a liar!

(ADMONIA *promptly presents her with another telegram.*)

LALA: This had better be an apology. (*To* ADMONIA.) Back up, darling. (*Reading*) "Dear Sadie, I'm not dead. P.S. Your child misses you." What? (*She squares off at the audience.*) Well, now, that does it! If you are my mother, which you are not. And this alleged child is my child, then that would mean I am a mother and I have never given birth. I don't know nothin' 'bout birthin' no babies! (*She laughs.*) Lala made a funny.

So whoever sent this, show me the child! Show me!

(ADMONIA *offers another telegram.*)

LALA: (*To* ADMONIA) You know you're gonna get fired! (*She reluctantly opens it.*) "The child is in the closet." What closet?

ADMONIA: Pst.

(ADMONIA *pushes a button and the center wall unit revolves around to reveal a large black door.* ADMONIA *exits, taking* FLO'RANCE *with her, leaving* LALA *alone.*)

LALA: (*Laughing*) I get it. It's a plot, isn't it. A nasty little CIA, FBI kind of plot. Well let me tell you muthafuckers one thing, there is nothing in that closet, real or manufactured, that will be a dimmer to the glimmer of Lamé the star. You may have gotten Billie and Bessie and a little piece of everyone else who's come along since, but you won't get Lala. My clothes are too fabulous! My hair is too long! My accent too French. That's why I came home to America. To prove you ain't got nothing on me!

(*The music for her next song starts, but* LALA *is caught up in her tirade, and talks/screams over the music.*)

My mother and Josephine Baker were French patriots together! I've had brunch with the Pope! I've dined with the Queen! Everywhere I go I cause riots! Hunny, I am a star! I have transcended pain! So there! (*Yelling*) Stop the music! Stop that goddamn music.

(*The music stops.* LALA *slowly walks downstage and singles out someone in the audience.*)

Darling, you're not looking at me. You're staring at that damn door. Did you pay to stare at some fucking door or be mesmerized by my talent?

(*To the whole audience:*)

Very well! I guess I am going to have to go to the closet door, fling it open, in order to dispell all the nasty little thoughts these nasty little telegrams have planted in your nasty little minds. (*Speaking directly to someone in the audience.*) Do you want me to open the closet door? Speak up, darling, this is live. (*Once she gets the person to say "yes."*) I will open the door, but before I do, let me tell you bastards one last thing. To hell with coming home and to hell with lies and insinuations!

(LALA *goes into the closet and after a short pause comes running out, ready to scream, and slams the door. Traumatized to the point of no return, she tells the following story as if it were a jazz solo of rushing, shifting emotions.*)

LALA: I must tell you this dream I had last night. Simply magnifique. In this dream, I'm running naked in Sammy Davis Junior's hair. (*Crazed laughter*)

Yes! I'm caught in this larger than life, deep, dark forest of savage, nappy-nappy hair. The kinky-kinks are choking me, wrapped around my naked arms, thighs, breast, face. I can't breathe. And there was nothing in that closet!

And I'm thinking if only I had a machete, I could cut away the kinks. Remove once and for all the roughness. But then I look up and it's coming toward me. Flowing like lava. It's pomade! Ohhh, Sammy!

Yes, cakes and cakes of pomade. Making everything nice and white and smooth and shiny, like my black/white/black/white/ black behiney.

Mama no!

And then spikes start cutting through the pomade. Combing the coated kink. Cutting through the kink, into me. There are bloodlines on my back. On my thighs.

It's all over. All over . . . all over me. All over for me.

(LALA *accidentally pulls off her wig to reveal her real hair. Stripped of her "disguise" she recoils like a scared little girl and sings.*)

MOMMY AND DADDY
MEET AND MATE
THE CHILD THAT'S BORN
IS TORN WITH LOVE AND WITH HATE
SHE RUNS AWAY TO FIND HER OWN
AND TRIES TO DENY
WHAT SHE'S ALWAYS KNOWN
THE GIRL INSIDE

(*The closet door opens.* LALA *runs away, and a* LITTLE BLACK GIRL *emerges from the closet. Standing behind her is* ADMONIA.)

(*The* LITTLE GIRL *and* LALA *are in two isolated pools of light, and mirror each other's moves until* LALA *reaches past her reflection and the* LITTLE GIRL *comes to* LALA *and they hug.* ADMONIA *then joins them as* LALA *sings. Music underscored.*)

LALA:
WHAT'S LEFT IS THE GIRL INSIDE
THE GIRL WHO DIED
SO A NEW GIRL COULD BE BORN

SLOW FADE TO BLACK

Permutations

(*Lights up on* NORMAL JEAN REYNOLDS. *She is very Southern/country and very young. She wears a simple faded print dress and her hair, slightly mussed, is in plaits. She sits, her dress covering a large oval object.*)

NORMAL: My mama used to say, God made the exceptional, then God made the special and when God got bored, he made me. 'Course she don't say too much of nuthin' no more, not since I lay me this egg.

(*She lifts her dress to uncover a large, white egg laying between her legs.*)

Ya see it all got started when I had me sexual relations with the garbage man. Ooowee, did he smell.

No, not bad. No! He smelled of all the good things folks never shoulda thrown away. His sweat was like cantaloupe juice. His neck was like a ripe-red strawberry. And the water that fell from his eyes was like a deep, dark, juicy-juicy grape. I tell ya, it was like fuckin' a fruit salad, only I didn't spit out the seeds. I kept them here, deep inside. And three days later, my belly commence to swell, real big like.

Well my mama locked me off in some dark room, refusin' to let me see light of day 'cause, "What would the neighbors think." At first I cried a lot, but then I grew used to livin' my days in the dark, and my nights in the dark. . . . (*She hums.*) And then it wasn't but a week or so later, my mama off at church, that I got this hurtin' feelin' down here. Worse than anything I'd ever known. And then I started bleedin', real bad. I mean there was blood everywhere. And the pain had me howlin' like a near-dead dog. I tell ya, I was yellin' so loud, I couldn't even hear myself. Noooooooo! Noooooo! Carrying on something like that.

And I guess it was just too much for the body to take, 'cause the next thing I remember . . . is me coming to and there's this big white egg layin' 'tween my legs. First I thought somebody musta put it there as some kind of joke. But then I noticed that all 'round this egg were thin lines of blood that I could trace to back between my legs.

(*Laughing*) Well, when my mama come home from church she just about died. "Normal Jean, what's that thing 'tween your legs? Normal Jean, you answer me, girl!" It's not a thing, Mama. It's an egg. And I laid it.

She tried separatin' me from it, but I wasn't havin' it. I stayed in that dark room, huggin', holdin' onto it.

And then I heard it. It wasn't anything that coulda been heard 'round the world, or even in the next room. It was kinda like layin' back in the bath tub, ya know, the water just coverin' your ears . . . and if you lay real still and listen real close, you can hear the sound of your heart movin' the water. You ever done that? Well that's what it sounded like. A heart movin' water. And it was happenin' inside here.

Why, I'm the only person I know who ever lay themselves an egg before so that makes me special. You hear that, Mama? I'm special and so's my egg! And special things supposed to be treated like they matter. That's why every night I count to it, so it knows nuthin' never really ends. And I sing it every song I know so that when it comes out, it's full of all kinds of feelings. And I tell it secrets and laugh with it and . . .

(*She suddenly stops and puts her ear to the egg and listens intently.*)

Oh! I don't believe it! I thought I heard . . . yes! (*Excited*) Can you hear it? Instead of one heart, there's two. Two little hearts just pattering away. Boom-boom-boom. Boom-boom-boom. Talkin' to each other like old friends. Racin' toward the beginnin' of their lives.

(*Listening*) Oh, no, now there's three . . . four . . . five, six. More hearts than I can count. And they're all alive, beatin' out life inside my egg.

(*We begin to hear the heartbeats, drums, alive inside* NORMAL*'s egg.*)

Any day now, this egg is gonna crack open and what's gonna come out a be the likes of which nobody has ever seen. My babies! And their skin is gonna turn all kinds of shades in the sun and their hair a be growin' every which-a-way. And it won't matter and they won't care 'cause they know they are so rare and so special 'cause it's not everyday a bunch of babies break outta a white egg and start to live.

And nobody better not try and hurt my babies 'cause if they do, they gonna have to deal with me.

Yes, any day now, this shell's gonna crack and my babies are gonna fly. Fly! Fly!

(*She laughs at the thought, but then stops and says the word as if it's the most natural thing in the world.*)

Fly.

BLACKOUT

The Party

(*Before we know what's hit us, a hurricane of energy comes bounding into the space. It is* TOPSY WASHINGTON. *Her hair and dress are a series of stylistic contradictions which are hip, black, and unencumbered.*)

(*Music, spiritual and funky, underscores.*)

TOPSY: (*Dancing about.*) Yoho! Party! Party! Turn up the music! Turn up the music!

Have yaw ever been to a party where there was one fool in the middle of the room, dancing harder and yelling louder than everybody in the entire place? Well, hunny, that fool was me!

Yes, child! The name is Topsy Washington and I love to party. As a matter of fact, when God created the world, on the seventh day, he didn't rest. No child, he P-A-R-T-I-E-D. Partied!

But now let me tell you 'bout this function I went to the other night, way uptown. And baby when I say way uptown, I mean way-way-way-way-way-way-way-way uptown. Somewhere's between 125th Street and infinity.

Inside was the largest gathering of black/Negro/colored Americans you'd ever want to see. Over in one corner you got Nat Turner sippin' champagne out of Eartha Kitt's slipper. And over in another corner, Bert Williams and Malcom X was discussing existentialism as it relates to the shuffle-ball-change. Girl, Aunt Jemima and Angela Davis was in the kitchen sharing a plate of greens and just goin' off about South Africa.

And then Fats sat down and started to work them eighty-eights.
And then Stevie joined in. And then Miles and Duke and Ella
and Jimi and Charlie and Sly and Lightin' and Count and
Louie!

And then everybody joined in. I tell you all the children was
just all up in there, dancing to the rhythm of one beat. Dancing
to the rhythm of their own definition. Celebrating in their cultural madness.

And then the floor started to shake. And the walls started to
move. And before anybody knew what was happening, the entire room lifted up off the ground. The whole place just took off
and went flying through space—defying logic and limitations.
Just a spinning and a spinning and a spinning until it disap-
peared inside of my head.

(TOPSY *stops dancing and regains her balance and begins to listen to
the music in her head. Slowly we begin to hear it, too.*)

That's right, girl, there's a party goin' on inside of here. That's
why when I walk down the street my hips just sashay all over
the place. 'Cause I'm dancing to the music of the madness in
me.

And whereas I used to jump into a rage anytime anybody tried
to deny who I was, now all I got to do is give attitude, quicker
than light, and then go on about the business of being me.
'Cause I'm dancing to the music of the madness in me.

(*As* TOPSY *continues to speak,* MISS ROJ, LALA, MISS PAT, *and* THE MAN
from SYMBIOSIS revolve on, frozen like soft sculptures.)

TOPSY: And here, all this time I been thinking we gave up our
    drums. But, naw, we still got 'em. I know I got mine. They're
    here, in my speech, my walk, my hair, my God, my style, my
    smile, and my eyes. And everything I need to get over in this
    world, is inside here, connecting me to everybody and every-
    thing that's ever been.

So, hunny, don't waste your time trying to label or define me.

(The sculptures slowly begin to come to "life" and they mirror/echo TOPSY's *words.)*

TOPSY/EVERYBODY: . . . 'cause I'm not what I was ten years ago or ten minutes ago. I'm all of that and then some. And whereas I can't live inside yesterday's pain, I can't live without it.

(All of a sudden, madness erupts on the stage. The sculptures begin to speak all at once. Images of black/Negro/colored Americans begin to flash—images of them dancing past the madness, caught up in the madness, being lynched, rioting, partying, surviving. Mixed in with these images are all the characters from the exhibits. Through all of this TOPSY *sings. It is a vocal and visual cacaphony which builds and builds.)*

LALA:
I must tell you about this dream I had last night. Simply magnifique. In this dream I'm running naked in Sammy Davis Junior's hair. Yes. I'm caught in this larger-than-life, deep, dark tangled forest of savage, nappy-nappy hair. Yes, the kinky kinks are choking me, are wrapped around my naked arms, my naked thighs, breast, and face, and I can't breathe and there was nothing in that closet.

MISS ROJ:
Snap for every time you walk past someone lying in the street smelling like frozen piss and shit and you don't see it. Snap for every crazed bastard who kills himself so as to get the jump on being killed. And snap for every sick muthafucker who, bored with carrying about his fear, takes to shooting up other people.

THE MAN:
I have no history. I have no past. I can't. It's too much. It's much too much. I must be able to smile on cue and watch the news with an impersonal eye. I have no stake in the madness. Being black is too emotionally

MISS PAT:
Stop playing those drums. I said stop playing those damn drums. You can't stop history. You can't stop time. Those drums will be confiscated once we reach Savannah, so give them up now. Repeat after me:

taxing, therefore I will be black only on weekends and holidays.   I don't hear any drums and I will not rebel. I will not rebel!

TOPSY: (*Singing*)
THERE'S MADNESS IN ME
AND THAT MADNESS SETS ME FREE
THERE'S MADNESS IN ME
AND THAT MADNESS SETS ME FREE
THERE'S MADNESS IN ME
AND THAT MADNESS SETS ME FREE
THERE'S MADNESS IN ME
AND THAT MADNESS SETS ME FREE
THERE'S MADNESS IN ME
AND THAT MADNESS SETS ME FREE

TOPSY: My power is in my . . .

EVERYBODY: *Madness!*

TOPSY: And my colored contradictions.

(*The sculptures freeze with a smile on their faces as we hear the voice of* MISS PAT.)

VOICE OF MISS PAT: Before exiting, check the overhead as any baggage you don't claim, we trash.

BLACKOUT

SPUNK

PRODUCTION HISTORY

Spunk was originally developed under the auspices of the Center Theatre Group of Los Angeles at the Mark Taper Forum, Gordon Davidson, Artistic Director. The play was funded in part by a grant from the Rockefeller Foundation.

Spunk had its world premiere at the Crossroads Theatre Company on November 2, 1989. Rick Khan was the Producing Artistic Director. George C. Wolfe directed the following cast:

GUITAR MAN	*Chic Street Man*
BLUES SPEAK WOMAN	*Betty K. Bynum*
THE FOLKS	*Danitra Vance, Reggie Montgomery, Kevin Jackson, Tico Wells*

Loy Arcenas designed the set; Toni-Leslie James, the costumes; Don Holder, the lighting; Hope Clarke, the choreography. David Horton Black was the Production Stage Manager. Sydné Mahone was the Dramaturg.

Spunk opened at Joseph Papp's New York Shakespeare Festival April 18, 1990 with George C. Wolfe directing the following cast:

GUITAR MAN	*Chic Street Man*
BLUES SPEAK WOMAN	*Ann Duquesnay*
THE FOLKS	*Danitra Vance, Reggie Montgomery, Kevin Jackson, K. Todd Freeman*

Loy Arcenas designed the set; Toni-Leslie James, the costumes; Don Holder, the lighting; Barbara Pollitt, the masks and puppets; Hope Clarke, the choreography. Jacqui Casto was the Production Stage Manager.

THE CHARACTERS

Blues Speak Woman
Guitar Man
The Folk, *an acting ensemble of three men and a woman*

TIME

"Round about long 'go"

PLACE

"O, way down nearby"

ACTING STYLE

It is suggested that the rhythms of the dialect be played, instead of the dialect itself. A subtle but important distinction. The former will give you Zora. The latter, Amos and Andy.

The emotional stakes of the characters in the three tales should not be sacrificed for "style." Nor should style be sacrificed because it gets in the way of the emotions. The preferred blend is one in which stylized gesture and speech are fueled by the emotional stakes.

SETTING

The setting is a playing arena, as stark as a Japanese woodcut and as elegant as the blues. The set piece for the three tales should be kept to a minimum so that gesture, lighting, music and the audience's imagination make the picture complete.

Note that throughout the third tale ("The Gilded Six-Bits"), the Players present props which are evocative of the story's shifting locales and time periods. The props should look playful, very used, yet magically simple.

ACT ONE

SYKES: Delta, is dat you Ah heah?
BLUES SPEAK WOMAN: She saw him on his hands and knees.
His horribly swollen neck, his one eye open, shining with . . .
SYKES: Hope.

Reggie Montgomery and Danitra Vance in "Sweat," from the 1990
New York Shakespeare Festival production of SPUNK.
Photo by Martha Swope

GIRL: You skillets is trying to promote a meal on me. But it'll never happen, brother. You barking up the wrong tree. I wouldn't give you air if you was stopped up in a jug. I'm not putting out a thing. I'm just like the cemetery. I'm not putting out, I'm takin' in. Dig. I'll tell you like the farmer told the potato—plant you now and dig you later. . . . Go ahead. Bedbug! Touch me! I'll holler like a pretty white woman!

The girl lets out three "pretty white woman" screams and then struts off.

K. Todd Freeman (left), Danitra Vance and Reggie Montgomery in "Story in Harlem Slang," from the 1990 New York Shakespeare Festival production of SPUNK.

Photo by Martha Swope

JOE: [Missie] had not seen the big tall man come stealing in the gate and creep up the walk grinning happily at the joyful mischief he was about to commit.

MISSIE: But she knew it was her husband throwing silver dollars in the door for her to pick up and pile beside her plate at dinner.

Danitra Vance with Kevin Jackson (kneeling) and K. Todd Freeman in "The Gilded Six-Bits," from the 1990 New York Shakespeare Festival production of SPUNK.

Photo by Martha Swope

WOMAN: . . . there were no more Saturday romps.
MAN: No ringing silver dollars to stack beside her plate.
MISSIE: No pockets to rifle.
WOMAN: In fact the yellow coin in his trousers was like a monster hiding in the cave of his pockets to destroy her.
MAN: She often wondered if he still had it but nothing could have induced her to ask nor explore his pockets to see for herself.
BOY: Its shadow was in the house whether or no.

From left to right, Reggie Montgomery, Anne Duquesnay, K. Todd Freeman, Kevin Jackson and Danitra Vance in "The Gilded Six-Bits," from the 1990 New York Shakespeare Festival production of SPUNK.
Photo by Martha Swope

MISS PAT: *(Placating)* OK, now I realize some of us are a bit edgy after hearing about the tragedy on board The Laughing Mary, but let me assure you Celebrity [Slaveship] has no intention of throwing you overboard and collecting the insurance. We value you! . . .
Why the songs you are going to sing in the cotton fields, under the burning heat and stinging lash, will metamorphose and give birth to the likes of James Brown and the Fabulous Flames. And you, yes *you,* are going to come up with some of the best dances. The best dances! The Watusi! The Funky Chicken! And just think of what *you* are going to mean to William Faulkner.

Danitra Vance in "Git on Board," from the 1986 New York Shakespeare Festival production of THE COLORED MUSEUM.
Photo by Martha Swope

MEDA: (*To* MAMA)
　Is good brother still going on and on and on
　about He and The Man.
MAMA/LADY: What else? . . .
SON: Girl, what has gotten into you?
MEDEA: Juilliard, good brother. For I am no
　longer bound by rhythms of race or

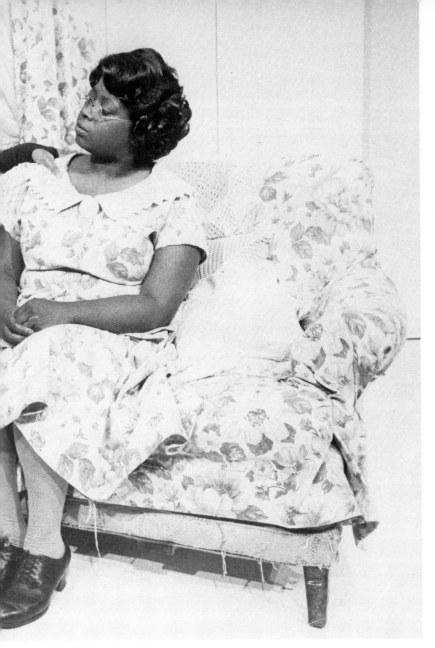

region. Oh, no. My speech, like my
pain and suffering, have become
classical and therefore universal.

Danitra Vance (left) with Vickilyn Reynolds in "The Last Mama-on-
the-Couch Play," from the 1986 New York Shakespeare Festival
production of THE COLORED MUSEUM.
Photo by Martha Swope

SOLDIER WITH A SECRET

JUNIE: . . . Guess what? I know a secret. The secret to your pain. 'Course I didn't always know. First I had to die, then come back to life, 'fore I had the gift . . . 'Cause just like Jesus went around healin' the sick, I'm supposed to go around healin' the hurtin' all these colored boys wearin' from the war.

Tommy Hollis in "Solider with a Secret," from the 1986 New York Shakespeare Festival production of THE COLORED MUSEUM.
Photo by Martha Swope

Prologue

(Lights reveal GUITAR MAN, *playing his guitar and whistling, signaling the tales are about to begin.* THE FOLK *casually enter, greeting one another. On a musical cue,* THE FOLK *freeze and* BLUES SPEAK WOMAN *struts on, singing with an earthy elegance.)*

SONG: GIT TO THE GIT

BLUES SPEAK WOMAN:
OOOOH . . .
HOW DO YOU GIT TO THE GIT?
GUITAR MAN:
HOW DO YOU GIT TO THE GIT?
BLUES SPEAK WOMAN:
I SAY,
HOW DO I GIT TO THE GIT?
GUITAR MAN:
YOU TELL 'EM
HOW TO GIT TO THE GIT?
BLUES SPEAK WOMAN:
WITH SO ME BLUES!
GUITAR MAN:
SOME BLUES!
BLUES SPEAK WOMAN:
N' SOME GRIT!
GUITAR MAN:
SOME GRIT!
BLUES SPEAK WOMAN:
SOME PAIN!
GUITAR MAN:
PAIN!
BLUES SPEAK WOMAN:
SOME SPIT!

GUITAR MAN:
   SPIT!
BLUES SPEAK WOMAN:
   N' SOME . . .
BLUES SPEAK WOMAN/GUITAR MAN:
   . . . SPUNK!
BLUES SPEAK WOMAN: How yaw doin'? (*With an attitude*) I said how
   yaw doin'? (*Once the audience responds correctly*) Well all right
   now! The name is Blues Speak Woman. N' this is Guitar Man.
   N' these are The Folk!

(THE FOLK *ceremoniously bow.*)

BLUES SPEAK WOMAN: Risk takers!

(*Presenting themselves.*)

WOMAN: Heart breakers!
MAN ONE: Masters of emotion!
MAN TWO: Masters of motion!
MAN THREE: N' makers of style.
BLUES SPEAK WOMAN: The three tales we are about to perform, cele-
   brate the laughin' kind of lovin' kind of hurtin' kind of pain that
   comes from bein' human. Tales of survival . . .

TOLD IN THE KEY OF THE BLUES.

Aww, take it away Mr. Guitar Man!

(*As* BLUES SPEAK WOMAN/GUITAR MAN *sing,* THE FOLK *don masks, and
utilizing dance/gesture, perform the following scenarios: a man and
a woman caught up in the playfulness of love.*)

GUITAR MAN:
   HEY-HEY HEY-HEY
   BABY HEY
BLUES SPEAK WOMAN:
   AWW GIMME SOME OF THAT SPUNK
GUITAR MAN:
   HEY-HEY, HEY-HEY
   BABY HEY

BLUES SPEAK WOMAN:
   AWW GIMME SOME OF THAT SPUNK
   YA GOTS TO GIMME
   GIMME SOME OF THAT SPUNK

(*The next scenario: a woman brushing off two men as they try to put the moves on her.*)

BLUES SPEAK WOMAN:
   NO! NO! NO! NO!
   WHAT I GOT YOU AIN'T GONNA GIT
GUITAR MAN:
   Come on now baby,
   Please don't be that way.
BLUES SPEAK WOMAN:
   I SAY NO! NO! NO! NO!
   WHAT I GOT YOU AIN'T GONNA GIT
GUITAR MAN:
   Baby please, I jes' wanna play.
BLUES SPEAK WOMAN:
   YO' HAIR MAY BE WAVY,
   YO' HEART IS JUST GRAVY
   WHAT I GOT YOU AIN'T GONNA GIT!
GUITAR MAN:
   NOW THESE FOLK RIDE IN A CADILLAC
   N' THOSE FOLK RIDE THE SAME
   BUT US FOLK RIDE IN A RUSTY FORD
   BUT WE GITS THERE JES' THE SAME

(*As* BLUES SPEAK WOMAN *continues to sing,* THE FOLK *set the stage for the first tale.*)

BLUES SPEAK WOMAN:
   AWWW LAUGHIN' . . .
   CRYIN'
   LOVIN'
   FEELIN' ALL KINDSA PAIN
   WILL GIT YOU TO THE GIT!

(*And then the last scenario: a man beating a woman down, until she has no choice but to submit.*)

BLUES SPEAK WOMAN (*Vocalizing the woman's emotions/pain*):
  AWWWW . . .
  AWWWW . . .
  AWWWW . . .

(*In isolated light.*)

  I GIT TO THE GIT
  WITH SOME PAIN N' SOME SPIT
  N' SOME SPUNK. . . .

(*The lights crossfade.*)

"Sweat"

(*Lights reveal* DELIA *posed over a washtub and surrounded by mounds of white clothes. Music underscore.*)

BLUES SPEAK WOMAN: It was eleven o'clock of a spring night in Florida. It was Sunday. Any other night Delia Jones would have been in bed . . .

DELIA (*Presenting herself*): But she was a washwoman.

BLUES SPEAK WOMAN:
AND MONDAY MORNING MEANT A GREAT DEAL
    TO HER.
So she collected the soiled clothes on Saturday, when she returned the clean things.

SUNDAY NIGHT AFTER CHURCH,

she would put the white things to soak.

SHE SQUATTED . . .
    SHE SQUATTED . . .

on the kitchen floor beside the great pile of clothes, sorting them into small heaps, and humming . . . humming a song in a joyful key . . .

DELIA: But wondering through it all where her husband, Sykes, had gone with her horse and buckboard.

(*Lights reveal* SYKES, *posed at the periphery of the playing arena, a bullwhip in his hand. As he creeps toward* DELIA . . .)

BLUES SPEAK WOMAN: Just then . . .
GUITAR MAN (*Taking up the chant*):
    SYKES . . .
    SYKES . . . (*Etc.*)

BLUES SPEAK WOMAN: Something long, round, limp and black fell upon her shoulders and slithered to the floor besides her.

DELIA: A great terror took hold of her!

BLUES SPEAK WOMAN: And then she saw, it was the big bullwhip her husband liked to carry when he drove.

DELIA: Sykes!

(*Music underscore ends. As the scene between* DELIA *and* SYKES *is played,* BLUES SPEAK WOMAN *and* GUITAR MAN *look on.*)

DELIA: Why you throw dat whip on me like dat? You know it would skeer me—looks just like a snake, an' you know how skeered Ah is of snakes.

SYKES (*Laughing*): Course Ah knowd it! That's how come Ah done it.

DELIA: You ain't got no business doing it.

SYKES: If you such a big fool dat you got to have a fit over a earth worm or a string, Ah don't keer how bad Ah skeer you.

DELIA (*Simultaneously*): Gawd knows it's a sin. Some day Ah'm gointuh drop dead from some of yo' foolishness. And another thing!

SYKES (*Mocking*): " 'Nother thing."

DELIA: Where you been wid mah rig? Ah feed dat pony. He ain't fuh you to be drivin' wid no bullwhip.

SYKES: You sho' is one aggravatin' nigger woman!

DELIA (*To the audience*): She resumed her work and did not answer him. (*Humming, she resumes sorting the clothes*)

SYKES: Ah tole you time and again to keep them white folks' clothes outa dis house.

DELIA: Ah ain't for no fuss t'night, Sykes. Ah just come from taking sacrament at the church house.

SYKES: Yeah, you just come from de church house on Sunday night. But heah you is gone to work on them white folks' clothes. You ain't nothing but a hypocrite. One of them amen-corner Christians. Sing, whoop and shout . . . (*Dancing on the clothes*) Oh Jesus! Have mercy! Help me Jesus! Help me!

DELIA: Sykes, quit grindin' dirt into these clothes! How can Ah git through by Sat'day if Ah don't start on Sunday?

SYKES: Ah don't keer if you never git through. Anyhow Ah done promised Gawd and a couple of other men, Ah ain't gointer have it in my house.

(DELIA *is about to speak.*)

SYKES: Don't gimme no lip either . . .

DELIA: Looka heah Sykes, you done gone too fur.

SYKES (*Overlapping*): . . . else Ah'll throw 'em out and put mah
fist up side yo' head to boot.

(DELIA *finds herself caught in* SYKES'S *grip.*)

DELIA: Ah been married to you fur fifteen years, and Ah been
takin' in washin' fur fifteen years. Sweat, sweat, sweat! Work
and sweat, cry and sweat, and pray and sweat.

SYKES: What's that got to do with me?

DELIA: What's it got to do with you, Sykes? (*She breaks free of
him*) Mah tub of suds is filled yo' belly with vittles more times
than yo' hands is filled it. Mah sweat is done paid for this house
and Ah reckon Ah kin keep on sweatin' in it. (*To the audience*)
She seized the iron skillet from the stove and struck a defensive
pose.

And that ole snaggle-toothed yella woman you runnin'
with ain't comin' heah to pile up on mah sweat and blood. You
ain't paid for nothin' on this place, and Ah'm gointer stay right
heah till Ah'm toted out foot foremost.

(*Musical underscore.* DELIA *maintains her ground, skillet in hand.*)

SYKES: Well, you better quit gittin' me riled up, else they'll be
totin' you out sooner than you expect. Ah'm so tired of you Ah
don't know whut to do. (*To the audience*) Gawd! How Ah hates
skinny wimmen.

(*He exits.*)

BLUES SPEAK WOMAN: A little awed by this new Delia, he sidled out
of the door and slammed the back gate after him. He did not
say where he had gone, but she knew too well. She knew very
well that he would not return until nearly daybreak. Her work
over, she went on to bed . . .

DELIA: But not to sleep at once. (*She envelops herself in a sheet,
which becomes her bed*)

BLUES SPEAK WOMAN: She lay awake, gazing upon the debris that cluttered their matrimonial trail. Not an image left standing along the way.

DELIA: Anything like flowers had long ago been drowned in the salty stream that had been pressed from her heart.

BLUES SPEAK WOMAN:
PRESSED FROM HER HEART.

DELIA: Her tears . . .

BLUES SPEAK WOMAN (*Echoing*):
TEARS.

DELIA: Her sweat . . .

BLUES SPEAK WOMAN:
SWEAT.

DELIA: Her blood . . .

BLUES SPEAK WOMAN:
HER BLOOD.

DELIA: She had brought love to the union . . .

BLUES SPEAK WOMAN: And he had brought a longing after the flesh.

DELIA: Two months after the wedding, he had given her the first brutal beating.

BLUES SPEAK WOMAN:
SHE WAS YOUNG AND SOFT THEN
SO YOUNG . . .
SO SOFT . . .

DELIA (*Overlapping*): But now she thought of her knotty, muscled limbs, her harsh knuckly hands, and drew herself up into an unhappy little ball . . .

BLUES SPEAK WOMAN:
IN THE MIDDLE OF THE BIG FEATHER BED

TOO LATE NOW FOR HOPE,

TOO LATE NOW FOR LOVE,
TOO LATE NOW TO HOPE FOR LOVE,
TOO LATE NOW FOR EVERYTHING

DELIA: Except her little home. She had built it for her old days, and planted one by one the trees and flowers there.

BLUES SPEAK WOMAN:
IT WAS LOVELY TO HER

DELIA: Lovely.

BLUES SPEAK WOMAN:
    LOVELY . . .

Somehow before sleep came, she found herself saying aloud—
DELIA: Oh well, whatever goes over the Devil's back, is got to
    come under his belly. Sometime or ruther, Sykes, like every-
    body else, is gonna reap his sowing.
BLUES SPEAK WOMAN: Amen! She went to sleep and slept.

(*Music underscore ends.*)

BLUES SPEAK WOMAN: Until he announced his presence in bed.

(SYKES *enters.*)

DELIA: By kicking her feet and rudely snatching the covers away.

(*As he grabs the sheet, blackout. Lights isolate* GUITAR MAN. *Music
underscore.*)

GUITAR MAN: People git ready for Joe Clarke's Porch. Cane
    chewin'! People watchin'! Nuthin' but good times, on Joe
    Clarke's Porch.

(*Lights reveal the men on the porch,* MAN ONE AND TWO. *Sitting
between them, a life-size puppet,* JOE CLARKE. *The men on the porch
scan the horizon, their movements staccato and stylized. Upon seeing an imaginary woman walk past . . .*)

MEN ON PORCH: Aww sookie! Sookie! Sookie! (*Ad lib*) Come here
    gal! Git on back here! Woman wait!

(*The "woman" continues on her way as the morning heat settles
in.*)

MAN TWO: It was a hot, hot day . . . near the end of July.
MAN ONE: The village men on Joe Clarke's porch even chewed cane
    . . . listlessly.
MAN TWO: What do ya say we . . . naw!
MAN ONE: How's about we . . . naw!
MAN TWO: Even conversation . . .

MAN ONE: Had collapsed under the heat.

(*Music underscore ends.*)

MAN TWO: "Heah come Delia Jones," Jim Merchant said, as the shaggy pony came 'round the bend of the road toward them.

MAN ONE: The rusty buckboard heaped with baskets of crisp, clean laundry.

MAN ONE/TWO: Yep.

MAN ONE: Hot or col', rain or shine, jes'ez reg'lar ez de weeks roll roun', Delia carries 'em an' fetches 'em on Sat'day.

MAN TWO: She better if she wanter eat. Sykes Jones ain't wuth de shot an' powder it would tek tuh kill 'em. Not to huh he ain't.

MAN ONE: He sho' ain't. It's too bad, too, cause she wuz a right pretty li'l trick when he got huh. Ah'd uh mah'ied huh mahself if he hadnter beat me to it.

(JOE CLARKE *scoffs at* MAN ONE'*s claim.*)

MAN ONE: That's the truth Joe.

BLUES SPEAK WOMAN: Delia nodded briefly at the men as she drove past.

(*The men tip their hats and bow.*)

MAN ONE/TWO: How ya do Delia.

MAN TWO: Too much knockin' will ruin any 'oman. He done beat huh 'nough tuh kill three women, let 'lone change they looks. How Sykes kin stommuck dat big, fat, greasy Mogul he's layin' roun' wid, gets me. What's hur name? Bertha?

MAN ONE: She's fat, thass how come. He's allus been crazy 'bout fat women. He'd a' been tied up wid one long time ago if he could a' found one tuh have him. Did Ah tell yuh 'bout him sidlin' roun' mah wife—bringin' her a basket uh pecans outa his yard fuh a present?

MAN TWO: There oughter be a law about him. He ain't fit tuh carry guts tuh a bear.

GUITAR MAN: Joe Clarke spoke for the first time.

(*Music underscore.*)

BLUES SPEAK WOMAN (*The voice of Joe Clarke*): Tain't no law on earth dat kin make a man be decent if it ain't in 'im.

MAN ONE/TWO (*Ad lib*): Speak the truth Joe. Tell it! Tell it!

BLUES SPEAK WOMAN (*As Joe Clarke*): Now-now-now, there's plenty men dat takes a wife lak dey a joint uh sugar-cane. It's round, juicy an' sweet when dey gits it. But dey squeeze an' grind, squeeze an' grind an' wring tell dey wrings every drop uh pleasure dat's in 'em out. When dey's satisfied dat dey is wrung dry . . .

MAN ONE: What dey do Joe?

BLUES SPEAK WOMAN (*As Joe Clarke*): Dey treats 'em jes' lak dey do a cane-chew. Throws 'em away! Now-now-now-now, dey knows whut dey's doin' while dey's at it, an' hates theirselves fur it. But they keeps on hangin' after huh tell she's empty. Den dey hates huh fuh bein' a cane-chew an' in de way.

MAN ONE: We oughter take Syke an' dat stray 'oman uh his'n down in Lake Howell swamp an' lay on de rawhide till they cain't say Lawd a' mussy.

MAN TWO: We oughter kill 'em!

MAN ONE: A grunt of approval went around the porch.

MEN: Umhmm, umhmm, umhmm.

MAN TWO: But the heat was melting their civic virtue.

MAN ONE: Elijah Mosley began to bait Joe Clarke.

Come on Joe, git a melon outa dere an' slice it up for yo' customers. We'se all sufferin' wid de heat. De bear's done got me!

BLUES SPEAK WOMAN (*As Joe Clarke*): Yaw gimme twenty cents and slice away.

MAN ONE/TWO (*Ad lib*): Twenty cents! I give you a nickel. Git it on out here Joe . . . (*Etc.*)

BLUES SPEAK WOMAN: The money was all quickly subscribed and the huge melon brought forth. At that moment . . .

SYKES: Sykes and Bertha arrived . . .

(BLUES SPEAK WOMAN *dons a hand-held mask and becomes* BERTHA.)

MAN ONE: A determined silence fell on the porch.

MAN TWO: And the melon was put away.

BLUES SPEAK WOMAN (*Lifting the Bertha mask*): Just then . . .

(DELIA *enters.*)

DELIA: Delia drove past on her way home, as Sykes . . .
SYKES: Was ordering magnificently for Bertha.

(*He kisses* BERTHA's *hand. She squeals.*)

SYKES: It pleased him for Delia to see this.
　　　Git whutsoever yo' heart desires, Honey. Give huh two
　bottles uh strawberry soda-water . . .

(BERTHA *squeals.*)

SYKES: Uh quart parched ground-peas . . .

(BERTHA *squeals.*)

SYKES: An' a block uh chewin' gum.
DELIA: With all this they left the store.
SYKES: Sykes reminding Bertha that this was his town . . .

(MAN ONE *makes a move to go after* SYKES. JOE CLARKE *restrains
him.*)

SYKES: And she could have it if she wanted it.

(*Music underscore ends. As* SYKES *and* BERTHA *exit* . . .)

MAN ONE: Where did Syke Jones git da stray 'oman from nohow?
MAN TWO: Ovah Apopka. Guess dey musta been cleanin' out de
　town when she lef'. She don't look lak a thing but a hunk uh
　liver wid hair on it.
MAN ONE (*Laughing*): Well, she sho' kin squall. When she gits
　ready tuh laff, she jes' opens huh mouf an' latches it back tuh de
　las' notch. No ole granpa alligator down in Lake Bell ain't got
　nothin' on huh.

(*Music underscore. In isolated pools of light, the men on the porch,*
DELIA *and* SYKES.)

GUITAR MAN:
　SWEAT . . .
　SWEAT . . .

BLUES SPEAK WOMAN: Bertha had been in town three months now.

MAN TWO: Sykes was still paying her room-rent at Della Lewis'.

MAN ONE: Naw!

MAN TWO: The only house in town that would have taken her in.

MAN ONE: Delia avoided the villagers and meeting places in her efforts to be blind and deaf.

MAN TWO: But Bertha nullified this to a degree, by coming to Delia's house to call Sykes out to her at the gate!

(DELIA *is seen listening as* SYKES *talks to the audience as if they were* BERTHA.)

SYKES: Sho' you kin have dat li'l ole house soon's Ah git dat 'oman outa dere. Everything b'longs tuh me an' you sho' kin have it. You kin git anything you wants. Dis is mah town an' you sho' kin have it.

BLUES SPEAK WOMAN:

THE SUN HAD BURNED JULY TO AUGUST
THE HEAT STREAMED DOWN
LIKE A MILLION HOT ARROWS
SMITING ALL THINGS LIVING UPON THE EARTH

Grass withered! Leaves browned! Snakes went blind in shedding! And men and dogs went mad. (*Eyeing* SYKES) Dog days.

GUITAR MAN:

SYKES . . .
SYKES . . .

(SYKES *surreptitiously places a wire-covered soap box, and covers it with the mound of clothes.*)

BLUES SPEAK WOMAN: Delia came home one day and found Sykes there before her. She noticed a soap box beside the steps, but paid no particular attention to it.

SYKES: Look in de box dere Delia, Ah done brung yuh somethin'.

BLUES SPEAK WOMAN: When she saw what it held . . .

(DELIA *crosses to the box and lifts the lid. Lights reveal the men on the porch. With rattlers in hand, they produce the sound of a snake's rattle.*)

DELIA: Syke! Syke, mah Gawd! You take dat rattlesnake 'way from heah! You gottuh. Oh Jesus, have mussy!

SYKES: Ah ain't got tuh do nuthin' uh de kin'—fact is Ah ain't got tuh do nuthin' but die.

(*Sound of the snake's rattle.*)

DELIA: Naw, now Syke, don't keep dat thing 'round tryin' tuh skeer me tuh death. You knows Ah'm even feared uh earth worms.

SYKES: Tain't no use uh you puttin' on airs makin' out lak you skeered uh dat snake. He wouldn't risk breakin' out his fangs 'gin yo' skinny laigs nohow. He's gointer stay right heah tell he die. Now he wouldn't bite me cause Ah knows how to handle 'im.

DELIA: Kill 'im Syke, please.

SYKES (*Staring transfixed into the box*): Naw, Ah ain't gonna kill it. Ah think uh damn sight mo' uh him dan you! Dat's a nice snake.

(SYKES *turns to find* DELIA *standing over him ready to strike him. He lifts the lid to the snake box—she backs away.*)

SYKES: An anybody doan lak it, kin jes' hit de grit.

BLUES SPEAK WOMAN: The snake stayed on.

MAN ONE: The snake stayed on.

MAN TWO: The snake stayed on.

(*As* DELIA *continues to speak,* SYKES *stalks the playing arena, waiting for her to "break."*)

DELIA: His box remained by the kitchen door. It rattled at every movement in the kitchen or the yard.

BLUES SPEAK WOMAN: One day Delia came down the kitchen steps. She saw his chalky-white fangs curved like scimitars hung in the wire meshes. This time she did not run away with averted eyes as usual. She stood for a long time in the doorway . . .

DELIA: In a red fury that grew bloodier for every second that she regarded the creature that was her torment.

BLUES SPEAK WOMAN: That night she broached the subject as soon as Sykes sat down to the table.

DELIA: Sykes!

(Music underscore ends. As the scene between DELIA *and* SYKES *is played,* BLUES SPEAK WOMAN *and* GUITAR MAN *look on.)*

DELIA: Ah wants you tuh take dat snake 'way fum heah. You done starved me an' Ah put up widcher. You done beat me an Ah took dat. But you done kilt all mah insides bringin' dat varmint heah.

SYKES (*To the audience*): Sykes poured out a saucer full of coffee and drank it deliberately before he answered.

A whole lot Ah keer 'bout how you feels inside uh out. Dat snake ain't goin' no damn wheah till Ah gets ready fuh 'im tuh go. So fur as beatin' is concerned, yuh ain't took near all dat you gointer take if yuh stay 'round me.

DELIA: Delia pushed back her plate and got up from the table.

Ah hates you, Sykes. Ah hates you tuh de same degree dat Ah useter love yuh. Ah done took an' took till mah belly is full up tuh mah neck. Dat's de reason Ah got mah letter fum de church an' moved mah membership tuh Woodbridge—so Ah don't haftuh take no sacrament wid yuh. Ah don't wantuh see yuh 'round me atall. Lay 'round wid dat 'oman all yuh wants tuh, but gwan 'way fum me an' mah house. Ah hates yuh lak uh suck-egg dog!

SYKES: Well, Ah'm glad you does hate me. Ah'm sho' tiahed uh you hangin' ontuh me. Ah don't want yuh. Look at yuh stringy ole neck! Yo' rawbony laigs an' arms is enough tuh cut uh man tuh death. You look jes' lak de devvul's doll-baby tuh me. You cain't hate me no worse dan Ah hates you. Ah been hatin' you fuh years.

DELIA: Yo' ole black hide don't look lak nothin' tuh me, but uh passle uh wrinkled up rubber, wid yo' big ole yeahs flappin' on each side lak uh paih uh buzzard wings. Don't think Ah'm gointuh be run 'way fum mah house neither. Ah'm goin' tuh de white folks 'bout you, mah young man, de very nex' time you lay yo' han's on me.

(She pushes him. He grabs her. She breaks free.)

DELIA: Mah cup is done run ovah!
Sykes departed from the house!

(SYKES *abruptly turns to exit, but his rage takes hold and he comes charging back, ready to hit her.*)

DELIA: Threatening her!

(*Just as he is about to hit* DELIA, *he stops, regains control of his emotions and gently kisses her.*)

SYKES (*Smiling*): But he made not the slightest move to carry out any of them.

(*He exits.*)

BLUES SPEAK WOMAN: That night he did not return at all. And the next day being Sunday . . .

(*Music underscore. Lights reveal the men on the porch, swaying to the gospel beat.*)

DELIA: Delia was glad she did not have to quarrel before she hitched up her pony and drove the four miles to Woodbridge.
BLUES SPEAK WOMAN: She stayed to the night service which was very warm and full of spirit. As she drove homeward she sang.
DELIA:
JURDEN WATER
BLUES SPEAK WOMAN/MEN ON PORCH:
JURDEN WATER
DELIA:
BLACK N' COLD
WOMAN/MEN:
BLACK N' COLD
DELIA:
CHILLS THE BODY
WOMAN/MEN:
CHILLS THE BODY
DELIA:
BUT NOT THE SOUL
WOMAN/MEN:
NOT THE SOUL
DELIA:
SAID I WANNA CROSS JURDEN

WOMAN/MEN:
> CROSS OVER JURDEN

DELIA:
> IN A CALM . . .

WOMAN/MEN:
> CALM TIME, CALM TIME, CALM TIME

DELIA:
> TIME . . .

(MEN *on porch repeat the "calm time" refrain as the action continues.*)

BLUES SPEAK WOMAN: She came from the barn to the kitchen door and stopped and addressed the snake's box.

DELIA: Whut's de mattah, ol' Satan, you ain't kickin' up yo' racket. (*She kicks the snake box*)

BLUES SPEAK WOMAN: Complete silence.

DELIA: Perhaps her threat to go to the white folks had frightened Sykes. Perhaps he was sorry.

BLUES SPEAK WOMAN: She decided she need not bring the hamper out of the bedroom; she would go in there and do the sorting. So she picked up the pot-bellied lamp and went in.

DELIA: The room was small and the hamper stood hard by the foot of the white iron bed.

BLUES SPEAK WOMAN (*A gospel riff*):
> SAID I WANTAH CROSS JURDEN

(MEN on porch/GUITAR MAN *add in.*)

WOMAN/MEN/GUITAR MAN:
> IN CALM . . .

(DELIA *screams.*)

DELIA: There lay the snake in the basket!

BLUES SPEAK WOMAN: She saw him pouring his awful beauty from the basket upon the bed. The wind from the open door blew out the light. She sped to the darkness of the yard, slamming the door after her before she thought to set down the lamp. She did not feel safe even on the ground. So she climbed up into the hay barn.

DELIA (*Sitting atop a ladder*): Finally she grew quiet. And with this stalked through her a cold, bloody rage. She went to sleep . . . a twitch sleep. And woke to a faint gray sky.

BLUES SPEAK WOMAN: There was a loud, hollow sound below. She peered out . . .

DELIA/BLUES SPEAK WOMAN: Sykes!

(SYKES *abruptly appears.*)

SYKES: . . . was at the wood-pile, demolishing a wire-covered box. He hurried to the kitchen door, but hung outside there some minutes before he entered and stood some minutes more inside before he closed it after him.

　　　　No mo' skinny women! No mo' white folks' clothes. This is my house! *My* house!

DELIA: Delia descended without fear now . . .

BLUES SPEAK WOMAN: And crouched beneath the low bedroom window. The drawn shade shut out the dawn, shut in the night, but the thin walls . . .

MAN ONE: Held . . .

MAN TWO: Back . . .

DELIA: No . . .

BLUES SPEAK WOMAN: Sound. Inside, Sykes heard nothing until he—

SYKES: Knocked a pot lid off the stove.

DELIA: Trying to reach the match-safe in the dark.

(*Music underscore.* MEN *on porch create sound of the snake rattle.* SYKES *stops dead in his tracks.*)

SYKES (*Leaping onto a chair*): Sykes made a quick leap into the bedroom.

BLUES SPEAK WOMAN: The rattling ceased for a moment as he stood . . .

SYKES: Paralyzed. He waited.

BLUES SPEAK WOMAN (*Sardonically*): It seemed that the snake waited also.

(*With regained composure,* SYKES *gets down from the chair and cautiously moves about.*)

SYKES: Where you at? Humm. Wherever that is, stay there while I . . .

DELIA: Sykes was muttering to himself . . .

BLUES SPEAK WOMAN: When the whirr began again.

(*Sound of snake's rattle and music underscore.*)

SYKES: Closer, right underfoot this time. He leaped—onto the bed.

(*In isolated light, the actor playing* SYKES *becomes both* SYKES *and the snake.*)

DELIA: Outside Delia heard a cry.

(SYKES *cries out in pain.*)

MAN ONE: A tremendous stir inside!

MAN TWO: Another series of animal screams!

(SYKES *cries out.*)

MAN ONE: A huge brown hand seizing the window stick!

MAN TWO: Great dull blows upon the wooden floor!

MAN ONE: Punctuating the gibberish of sound long after the rattle of the snake . . .

MAN TWO: Had abruptly subsided.

(*Music underscore ends.*)

BLUES SPEAK WOMAN: All this Delia could see and hear from her place beneath the window. And it made her ill. She crept over to the four-o'clocks and stretched herself on the cool earth to recover.

(*Music underscore. As* BLUES SPEAK WOMAN *talks/sings,* SYKES *crawls toward* DELIA. *Meanwhile, the* MEN *on the porch scan the horizon, signaling the beginning of a new day.*)

BLUES SPEAK WOMAN: She lay there. She could hear Sykes . . .

CALLING IN A MOST DESPAIRING TONE

As one who expected no answer.

THE SUN CREPT ON UP . . .

And he called.
Delia could not move. She never moved.
He called

AND THE SUN KEPT ON RISIN'
  "MAH GAWD!"
SHE HEARD HIM MOAN
  "MAH GAWD FROM HEBBEN."

She heard him stumbling about and got up from her flower bed.

THE SUN WAS GROWING WARM.

(*The music ends.*)

SYKES: Delia, is dat you Ah heah?
BLUES SPEAK WOMAN: She saw him on his hands and knees. His
  horribly swollen neck, his one eye open, shining with . . .
SYKES: Hope.

(SYKES *extends his hand toward* DELIA. *The weight and desperation
of his grip pulls her to the ground. She is about to console him, but
instead, scurries away.*)

DELIA: A surge of pity too strong to support bore her away from
  that eye . . .
BLUES SPEAK WOMAN: That must, could not, fail to see the lamp.
DELIA: Orlando with its doctors . . .
BLUES SPEAK WOMAN: Oh it's too far!

(SYKES *grabs hold to the hem of her dress.* DELIA *calmly steps beyond his reach.*)

DELIA: She could scarcely reach the chinaberry tree, where she
  waited . . . in the growing heat . . .

BLUES SPEAK WOMAN: While inside she knew, the cold river was creeping up . . . creeping up to extinguish that eye which must know by now that she knew.

(*Music underscore.* DELIA *looks on as* SYKES *recoils into a fetal position and dies. The sound of the snake's rattle as she looks at the audience.*)

DELIA: Sweat!

(*Blackout.*)

SONG: I'VE BEEN LIVING WITH THE BLUES

(*In isolated light,* GUITAR MAN.)

GUITAR MAN: Not everybody's got a snake in they house, but we all gits the blues.

ROCKS IS MY PILLOW
COLD GROUND MY BED
BLUE SKIES MY BLANKET
MOONLIGHT MY SPREAD
I'M NOT ASHAMED
AIN'T THAT NEWS
I BEEN LIVIN' WITH THE BLUES

I WORKS ALL SUMMER
I SLEEPS ALL FALL
I SPEND MY CHRISTMAS
IN MY OVERALLS
I'M NOT ASHAMED
HONEY AIN'T THAT NEWS
I BEEN LIVIN' WITH THE BLUES

(*Music interlude.*)

OOH, ROCKS HAS BEEN MY PILLOW
COLD GROUND HAS BEEN MY BED

BLUE SKIES HAVE BEEN MY BLANKET
AND THE MOONLIGHT HAS BEEN MY SPREAD

IF YOU'VE EVER BEEN DOWN
YOU KNOW JUST HOW I FEEL
I FEEL LIKE AN ENGINE
GOT NO DRIVIN' WHEEL

I'M NOT ASHAMED
NUTHIN' NEW
I BEEN LIVIN' WITH THE BLUES

MY MOMMA HAD 'EM
MY DADDY HAD 'EM TOO
YES HE DID
YOU SEE, I BEEN LIVIN' WITH THE BLUES

ALL YOU PEOPLE
OUT THERE TOO
YES YOU HAVE
WE ALL BEEN LIVIN' WITH THE BLUES

(*Three panels, suggestive of 1940s Harlem, drop onto the stage.* BLUES SPEAK WOMAN *struts on, her accessories and attitude are Harlem highbrow, with a touch of the "low."* GUITAR MAN *likes what he sees, and so the game begins.*)

SONG: HEY BABY
GUITAR MAN:
    HEY BABY,
    SAY BABY HOW DO YOU DO?
BLUES SPEAK WOMAN: You talkin' to me?
GUITAR MAN:
    YEAH BABY,
    SAY BABY HOW DO YOU DO?
    TELL ME HOW DO YOU DO
    SO I CAN DO A LITTLE BIT WITH YOU
BLUES SPEAK WOMAN: Do what with who?
GUITAR MAN: With you sweet mama, with you.
BLUES SPEAK WOMAN (*Walking toward him*):
    YEAH I'M LOOKIN',
    LOOKIN' EVERYWHERE I GO

YEAH I'M LOOKIN',
LOOKIN' BOTH HIGH N' LOW
AND WHEN I LOOK AT YOU . . .
GUITAR MAN: What you see baby?
BLUES SPEAK WOMAN:
   I SEE I GOTS TO LOOK SOME MO'!

(She walks away. He calls after her.)

GUITAR MAN:
   HEY BABY,
   WHO DO YOU THINK I AM?
BLUES SPEAK WOMAN:
   HEY BABY,
   WHO DO YOU THINK I AM?
   I'M JUST A FINE FRAIL RAIL
GUITAR MAN:
   AND I'M HOT AS JULY JAM

(Moving in for the kill)

   HEY BABY,
   I'D LIKE TO LAY NOW NEXT TO YOU
BLUES SPEAK WOMAN:
   WELL, MAYBE,
   I'D LIKE TO . . . NEXT TO YOU TOO
BLUES SPEAK WOMAN/GUITAR MAN:
   BUT I'M SO GOOD LOOKIN'
BLUES SPEAK WOMAN:
   I SAID I'M GOOD LOOKIN'
GUITAR MAN:
   I'M GOOD LOOKIN'!
BLUES SPEAK WOMAN: Don't you bull-skate me baby cause just
   look at this! Look at this! If you lookin' for a dusty
   butt, Beluthahatchie is that way 'n' that way. Any way but this
   way.

   CAUSE IT DON'T GIT!
   NO IT DON'T GIT
   IT DON'T GIT NO BETTER . . . THAN THIS

GUITAR MAN: No baby, don't *you* bull-skate *me*. Cause I'm fine as wine. I say I'm fine as wine. Randy, dandy and handy, smooth like brandy.

I COME ON LIGHTLY
SLIGHTLY . . .
AND OOOOOOH, SO POLITELY
IN OTHER WORDS . . .
BLUES SPEAK WOMAN/GUITAR MAN:
I'M TOO GOOD LOOKIN' FOR YOU!

(*They turn to go in opposite directions, stop and then look back.*)

BLUES SPEAK WOMAN/GUITAR MAN: But then again . . .

(*Fade to black.*)

TALE NUMBER TWO

"Story in
Harlem Slang"

(*Lights reveal* SLANG TALK MAN: *his attire, very debonair; his manner of speaking, very smooth.*)

SLANG TALK MAN: Wait till I light up my coal-pot and tell you about this Zigaboo called Jelly.

(*On* SLANG TALK MAN's *signal, lights reveal* JELLY, *a hick trying to pass himself off as slick. He wears a stocking cap and underneath his "street" bravado is a boyish charm.*)

JELLY: Well all right now!
SLANG TALK MAN: He was sealskin brown and papa-tree-top tall.
JELLY: Skinny in the hips and solid built for speed.
SLANG TALK MAN: He was born with this rough-dried hair, but when he laid on the grease and pressed it down overnight with his stocking-cap . . .

(JELLY *pulls off the cap to admire his "do."*)

JELLY: It looked just like righteous moss.
SLANG TALK MAN: Had so many waves, you got seasick from lookin'.
JELLY: Solid man solid.
SLANG TALK MAN: His mama named him Marvel, but after a month on Lenox Avenue . . .

(*On* SLANG TALK MAN's *signal, a zoot-suit jacket and hat magically appear.*)

SLANG TALK MAN: He changed all that to—
JELLY (*Getting dressed*): Jelly.
SLANG TALK MAN: How come? Well he put it in the street that when it comes to filling that long-felt need . . .

JELLY: Sugar-curing the ladies' feelings . . .

SLANG TALK MAN: He was in a class by himself. And nobody knew his name, so he had to tell 'em.

JELLY: It must be Jelly cause jam don't shake!

SLANG TALK MAN: That was what was on his sign. The stuff was there and it was mellow. N' whenever he was challenged by a hard-head or a frail eel on the right of his title, he would eyeball the idol-breaker with a slice of ice and say—

JELLY: Youse just dumb to the fact, baby. If you don't know what you talking 'bout, you better ask Granny Grunt. I wouldn't mislead you baby. I don't need to. Not with the help I got.

SLANG TALK MAN: Then he would give the pimp's sign . . .

(JELLY/SLANG TALK MAN *adopt an exaggerated "street" pose; for* SLANG TALK MAN *it's empty posturing; for* JELLY *it's the real deal.*)

SLANG TALK MAN: And percolate on down the Avenue.

(*On* SLANG TALK MAN's *signal, the* FOOTNOTE VOICE *is heard. As the* VOICE *speaks,* JELLY *practices a series of poses.*)

FOOTNOTE VOICE: Please note. In Harlemese, pimp has a different meaning than its ordinary definition. The Harlem pimp is a man whose amatory talents are for sale to any woman who will support him, either with a free meal or on a common-law basis; in this sense, he is actually a male prostitute.

SLANG TALK MAN: So this day he was airing out on the Avenue. It had to be late afternoon, or he would not have been out of bed.

JELLY: Shoot, all you did by rolling out early was to stir your stomach up. (*Confidentially*) That made you hunt for more dishes to dirty. The longer you slept, the less you had to eat.

SLANG TALK MAN: But you can't collar nods all day. So Jelly . . .

(*Music underscore.*)

SLANG TALK MAN: Got into his zoot suit with the reet pleats and got out to skivver around and do himself some good.

(*The transformation from "Jelly the Hick" into "Jelly the Slick" is now complete. He struts and poses like a tiger on the prowl; his moves suggestive, arrogant, mocking.*)

Lights reveal BLUES SPEAK WOMAN *and* GUITAR MAN, *sitting outside the playing arena, scatting vocalise which accents* JELLY'*s moves.*)

JELLY: No matter how long you stay in bed, and how quiet you keep, sooner or later that big guts is going to reach over and grab that little one and start to gnaw. That's confidential from the Bible. You got to get out on the beat and collar yourself a hot!

SLANG TALK MAN: At 132nd Street, he spied one of his colleagues, Sweet Back! Standing on the opposite sidewalk, in front of a café.

(*Lights reveal* SWEET BACK, older than JELLY; *the wear and tear of the street is starting to reveal itself in* SWEET BACK'*s face. Nonetheless, he moves with complete finesse as he and* JELLY *stalk each other, each trying to outdo the other as they strut, pose and lean.*)

SLANG TALK MAN: Jelly figured that if he bull-skated just right, he might confidence Sweet Back out of a thousand on a plate. Maybe a shot of scrap-iron or a reefer. Therefore, they both took a quick backward look at the soles of their shoes to see how their leather was holding out. They then stanched out into the street and made the crossing.

(*Music underscore ends.*)

JELLY: Hey there, Sweet Back. Gimme some skin!

SWEET BACK: Lay the skin on me pal. Ain't seen you since the last time, Jelly. What's cookin'?

JELLY: Oh, just like the bear, I ain't no where. Like the bear's brother, I ain't no further. Like the bear's daughter, ain't got a quarter.

SLANG TALK MAN: Right away he wished he had not been so honest. Sweet Back gave him a—

SWEET BACK: Top-superior, cut-eye look.

SLANG TALK MAN: Looked at Jelly just like—

SWEET BACK: A showman looks at an ape.

SLANG TALK MAN: Just as far above Jelly as fried chicken is over branch water.

SWEET BACK: Cold in the hand huh? A red hot pimp like you say you is ain't got no business in the barrel. Last night when I left you, you was beating up your gums and broadcasting about how hot you was. Just as hot as July jam, you told me. What you doin' cold in hand?

JELLY: Aw man, can't you take a joke? I was just beating up my gums when I said I was broke. How can I be broke when I got the best woman in Harlem? If I ask her for a dime, she'll give me a ten dollar bill. Ask her for a drink of likker, and she'll buy me a whiskey still. If I'm lyin' I'm flyin'!

SWEET BACK: Man, don't hang out that dirty washing in my back yard. Didn't I see you last night with that beat chick, scoffing a hot dog? That chick you had was beat to the heels. Boy, you ain't no good for what you live. And you ain't got nickel one. (*As if to a passing woman*) Hey baby!

SLANG TALK MAN: Jelly—

JELLY: Threw back the long skirt of his coat.

SLANG TALK MAN: And rammed his hand into his pants pocket. Sweet Back—

SWEET BACK: Made the same gesture . . .

SLANG TALK MAN: Of hauling out non-existent money.

JELLY: Put your money where your mouth is. Back yo' crap with your money. I bet you five dollars.

SWEET BACK: Oh yeah!

JELLY: Yeah.

(JELLY/SWEET BACK *move toward each other, wagging their pants pockets at each other.*)

SWEET BACK (*Playfully*): Jelly-Jelly-Jelly. I been raised in the church. I don't bet. But I'll doubt you. Five rocks!

JELLY: I thought so. (*Loud talking*) I knowed he'd back up when I drawed my roll on him.

SWEET BACK: You ain't drawed no roll on me, Jelly. You ain't drawed nothing but your pocket. (*With an edge*) You better stop that boogerbooing. Next time I'm liable to make you do it.

SLANG TALK MAN: There was a splinter of regret in Sweet Back's voice. If Jelly really had had some money, he might have staked him to a hot.

SWEET BACK: Good Southern cornbread with a piano on a platter.

SLANG TALK MAN: Oh well! The right broad would . . . might come along.

JELLY: Who boogerbooing? Jig, I don't have to. Talkin' about me with a beat chick scoffing a hot dog? Man you musta not seen me, 'cause last night I was riding 'round in a Yellow Cab, with a yellow gal, drinking yellow likker and spending yellow money. (*To the audience*) Tell 'em 'bout me. You was there. Tell 'em!

SWEET BACK: Git out of my face Jelly! That broad I seen you with wasn't no pe-ola. She was one of them coal-scuttle blondes with hair just as close to her head as ninety-nine to hundred. She look-ted like she had seventy-five pounds of clear bosom, and she look-ted like six months in front and nine months behind. Buy you a whiskey still! That broad couldn't make the down payment on a pair of sox.

JELLY: Naw-naw-naw-now Sweet Back, long as you been knowing me, you ain't never seen me with nothing but pe-olas. I can get any frail eel I wants to. How come I'm up here in New York? Huh-huh-huh? You don't know, do you? Since youse dumb to the fact, I reckon I'll have to make you hep. I had to leave from down south cause Miss Anne used to worry me so bad to go with her. Who me? Man, I don't deal in no coal.

SWEET BACK: Aww man, you trying to show your grandma how to milk ducks. Best you can do is confidence some kitchen-me-chanic out of a dime or two. Me, I knocks the pad with them cackbroads up on Sugar Hill and fills 'em full of melody. Man, I'm quick death 'n' easy judgment. You just a home-boy, Jelly. Don't try to follow me.

JELLY: Me follow you! Man, I come on like the Gang Busters and go off like The March of Time. If that ain't so, God is gone to Jersey City and you know He wouldn't be messing 'round a place like that.

SLANG TALK MAN: Looka there!

(SWEET BACK/JELLY *scurry and look.*)

SLANG TALK MAN: Oh well, the right broad might come along.

JELLY: Know what my woman done? We hauled off and went to church last Sunday. And when they passed 'round the plate for the penny collection, I throwed in a dollar. The man looked at me real hard for that. That made my woman mad, so she called him back and throwed in a twenty dollar bill. Told him to take that and go! That's what he got for looking at me 'cause I throwed in a dollar.

SWEET BACK: Jelly . . .
  The wind may blow
  And the door may slam.
  That what you shooting
  Ain't worth a damn!
JELLY: Sweet Back you fixing to talk out of place.
SWEET BACK: If you tryin' to jump salty Jelly, that's yo' mammy.
JELLY: Don't play in the family Sweet Back. I don't play the doz-
  ens. I done told you.
SLANG TALK MAN: Jelly—
JELLY: Slammed his hand in his bosom as if to draw a gun.
SLANG TALK MAN: Sweet Back—
SWEET BACK: Did the same.
JELLY: If you wants to fight, Sweet Back, the favor is in me.

(JELLY/SWEET BACK *begin to circle one another, each waiting on the other to "strike" first.*)

SWEET BACK: I was deep-thinking then, Jelly. It's a good thing I
  ain't short-tempered. Tain't nothing to you nohow.
JELLY: Oh yeah. Well, come on.
SWEET BACK: No you come on.
SWEET BACK/JELLY (*Overlapping*): Come on! Come on! Come on!
  Come on!

(*They are now in each other's face, grimacing, snarling, ready to fight, when* SWEET BACK *throws* JELLY *a look.*)

SWEET BACK: You ain't hit me yet.

(*They both begin to laugh, which grows, until they are falling all over each other: the best of friends.*)

SWEET BACK: Don't get too yaller on me Jelly. You liable to get
  hurt some day.
JELLY: You over-sports your hand yo' ownself. Too blamed astorperious. I just don't pay you no mind. Lay the skin on me
  man.
SLANG TALK MAN: They broke their handshake hurriedly, because
  both of them looked up the Avenue and saw the same thing.
SWEET BACK/JELLY: It was a girl.

(*Music underscore as lights reveal the girl, busily posing and preening.*)

SLANG TALK MAN: And they both remembered that it was Wednesday afternoon. All the domestics off for the afternoon with their pay in their pockets.

SWEET BACK/JELLY: Some of them bound to be hungry for love.

SLANG TALK MAN: That meant . . .

SWEET BACK: Dinner!

JELLY: A shot of scrap-iron!

SWEET BACK: Maybe room rent!

JELLY: A reefer or two!

SLANG TALK MAN: They both . . .

SWEET BACK: Went into the pose.

JELLY: And put on the look. (*Loud talking*) Big stars falling.

SLANG TALK MAN: Jelly said out loud when the girl was in hearing distance.

JELLY: It must be just before day!

SWEET BACK: Yeah man. Must be recess in Heaven, pretty angel like that out on the ground.

SLANG TALK MAN: The girl drew abreast of them, reeling and rocking her hips.

(BLUES SPEAK WOMAN *scats as the* GIRL *struts, her hips working to the beat of the music.* JELLY *and* SWEET BACK *swoop in and begin their moves.*)

JELLY: I'd walk clear to Diddy-Wah-Diddy to get a chance to speak to a pretty li'l ground-angel like that.

SWEET BACK: Aw, man you ain't willing to go very far. Me, I'd go slap to Ginny-Gall, where they eat cow-rump, skin and all.

SLANG TALK MAN: The girl smiled, so Jelly set his hat and took the plunge.

JELLY: Ba-by, what's on de rail for de lizard?

SLANG TALK MAN: The girl halted and braced her hips with her hands.

(*Music underscore stops.*)

GIRL: A Zigaboo down in Georgy, where I come from, asked a woman that one time and the judge told him ninety days.

(*Music underscore continues.*)

SWEET BACK: Georgy! Where 'bouts in Georgy you from? Delaware?

JELLY: Delaware? My people! My people! Man, how you going to put Delaware in Georgy. You ought to know that's in Maryland.

(*Music underscore stops.*)

GIRL: Oh, don't try to make out youse no northerner, you! Youse from right down in 'Bam your ownself.

JELLY: Yeah, I'm *from* there and I aims to stay from there.

GIRL: One of them Russians, eh? Rushed up here to get away from a job of work.

(*Music underscore continues.*)

SLANG TALK MAN: That kind of talk was not leading towards the dinner table.

JELLY: But baby! That shape you got on you! I bet the Coca-Cola company is paying you good money for the patent!

SLANG TALK MAN: The girl smiled with pleasure at this, so Sweet Back jumped in.

SWEET BACK: I know youse somebody swell to know. Youse real people. There's dickty jigs 'round here tries to smile. You grins like a regular fellow.

SLANG TALK MAN: He gave her his most killing look and let it simmer.

SWEET BACK: S'pose you and me go inside the café here and grab a hot.

(*Music underscore ends.*)

GIRL: You got any money?

SLANG TALK MAN: The girl asked and stiffed like a ramrod.

GIRL: Nobody ain't pimping on me. You dig me?

SWEET BACK/JELLY: Aww now baby!

GIRL: I seen you two mullet-heads before. I was uptown when Joe Brown had you all in the go-long last night. That cop sure hates a pimp. All he needs to see is the pimps' salute and he'll out

with his night-stick and ship your head to the red. Beat your
head just as flat as a dime.

(*The* GIRL *sounds off like a siren.* SWEET BACK *and* JELLY *rush to
silence her.*)

SWEET BACK: Ah-ah-ah, let's us don't talk about the law. Let's talk
about us. About you goin' inside with me to holler, "Let one
come flopping! One come grunting! Snatch one from the rear!"
GIRL: Naw indeed. You skillets is trying to promote a meal on me.
But it'll never happen, brother. You barking up the wrong tree.
I wouldn't give you air if you was stopped up in a jug. I'm not
putting out a thing. I'm just like the cemetery. I'm not putting
out, I'm takin' in. Dig. I'll tell you like the farmer told the
potato—plant you now and dig you later.

(*Music underscore.*)

SLANG TALK MAN: The girl made a movement to switch off. Sweet
Back had not dirtied a plate since the day before. He made a
weak but desperate gesture.

(*Just as* SWEET BACK *places his hand on her purse, the* GIRL *turns to
stare him down. Music underscore ends.*)

GIRL: Trying to snatch my pocketbook, eh?
SLANG TALK MAN: Instead of running . . .

(*The* GIRL *grabs* SWEET BACK*'s zoot-suit jacket.*)

GIRL: How much split you want back here? If your feets don't
hurry up and take you 'way from here, you'll ride away. I'll
spread my lungs all over New York and call the law.

(JELLY *moves in to try and calm her.*)

GIRL: Go ahead. Bedbug! Touch me! I'll holler like a pretty white
woman!

(*The* GIRL *lets out three "pretty white woman" screams and then
struts off. Music underscores her exit.*)

SLANG TALK MAN: She turned suddenly and rocked on off, her earring snapping and her heels popping.

SWEET BACK: My people, my people.

SLANG TALK MAN: Jelly made an effort to appear that he had no part in the fiasco.

JELLY: I know you feel chewed.

SWEET BACK: Oh let her go. When I see people without the periodical principles they's supposed to have, I just don't fool with 'em. (*Calling out after her*) What I want to steal her old pocketbook with all the money I got? I could buy a beat chick like you and give you away. I got money's mammy and Grandma's change. One of my women, and not the best one I got neither, is buying me ten shag suits at one time.

He glanced sidewise at Jelly to see if he was convincing.

JELLY: But Jelly's thoughts were far away.

(*Music underscore.*)

SLANG TALK MAN: He was remembering those full hot meals he had left back in Alabama to seek wealth and splendor in Harlem without working. He had even forgotten to look cocky and rich.

BLUES SPEAK WOMAN:
I GIT TO THE GIT
WITH SOME PAIN AND SOME SPIT
AND SOME SPUNK

(*The lights slowly fade.*)

ACT TWO

SONG: YOU BRINGS OUT THE BOOGIE IN ME

(*Lights reveal* BLUES SPEAK WOMAN *and* GUITAR MAN.)

BLUES SPEAK WOMAN:
   I DON'T KNOW WHAT YOU GOT
   BUT IT DON'T TAKE A GENIUS TO SEE
   BUT WHATEVER YOU GOT
   IT'S HOT AND IT'S MELTING ME
GUITAR MAN: Don't hurt yo'self now.
BLUES SPEAK WOMAN:
   WHEN YOU UMMMM LIKE THAT
   AND YOU AHHHH LIKE THAT
   YOU CAN MAKE ME CLIMB DOWN FROM MY TREE
   YOUR LOVE HAS SHOOK ME UP
   AND IT BRINGS OUT THE BOOGIE IN ME
GUITAR MAN:
   ALL THE WOMEN I HAD
   THEY WERE GLAD WHEN MY BOOGIE GOT TIRED
BLUES SPEAK WOMAN: Ohhh your boogie is callin' me home.
GUITAR MAN:
   THEY WOULD SPUTTER AND SCRATCH
   LIKE A MATCH THAT YOU CAN'T SET ON FIRE
   WHEN YOU OOOOHH LIKE THAT
   AND YOU OHHHH LIKE THAT
   YOU CAN MAKE A BLIND MAN SEE
   YOU'RE A CHOCOLATE COOKIE
   AND YOU BRING OUT THE BOOGIE IN ME

(*They scat.*)

GUITAR MAN:
   LET'S GO DOWN TO THE BEACH
   YOU COULD TEACH ME A THING OR TWO

BLUES SPEAK WOMAN:
  WE COULD SPEND ALL OUR TIME
  DRINKIN' WINE IN MY RED TIP CANOE
BLUES SPEAK WOMAN/GUITAR MAN:
  WE COULD UMMMMM . . . LIKE THIS
  WE COULD AHHHHHHH . . . LIKE THIS
  WE COULD SHAKE THE FRUIT DOWN FROM THE
    TREE
  YOUR LOVE HAS SHOOK ME UP
  AND IT BRINGS OUT THE BOOGIE IN ME
BLUES SPEAK WOMAN:
  YOUR LOVE HAS SHOOK ME UP
  AND IT BRINGS OUT THE BOOGIE IN ME
GUITAR MAN:
    YOUR LOVE HAS SHOOK ME UP
    AND IT BRINGS OUT THE BOOGIE IN ME
BLUES SPEAK WOMAN/GUITAR MAN:
  YOUR LOVE HAS SHOOK ME UP
  AND IT BRINGS OUT THE BOOGIE IN ME!
GUITAR MAN:
  YOUR LOVE
  YOUR LOVE
BLUES SPEAK WOMAN (*Simultaneously*):
  YOU KNOW IT SHOOK ME
  IT REALLY SHOOK ME UP
GUITAR MAN:
    BRINGS OUT THE BOOGIE
BLUES SPEAK WOMAN:
    BRINGS OUT THE BOOGIE
BLUES SPEAK WOMAN/GUITAR MAN:
    BRINGS OUT THE BOOGIE
    IN ME!

(*Blackout.*)

TALE NUMBER THREE

"The Gilded Six-Bits"

(*Music underscore. Lights reveal the* PLAYERS, *a trio of vaudevillians. They present themselves to the audience.* THE MAN *speaks with a grandioso eloquence.* THE WOMAN (*played by* BLUES SPEAK WOMAN) *is voluptuous and refined.* THE BOY, *their assistant, is awkward yet willing. On the* MAN's *cue, the tale begins.*)

MAN: It was a Negro yard, around a Negro house, in a Negro settlement that looked to the payroll of the G and G Fertilizer works for its support. But there was something happy about the place.

WOMAN: The front yard was parted in the middle by a sidewalk from gate to doorstep.

MAN: A mess of homey flowers . . .

(*The* WOMAN *flashes her floral fan, which becomes the planted flowers.*)

MAN: . . . planted without a plan bloomed cheerily from their helter-skelter places.

WOMAN: The fence and house were whitewashed. The porch and steps scrubbed white.

BOY: It was Saturday.

WOMAN: Everything clean from the front gate to the privy house.

MAN: Yard raked so that the strokes of the rake would make a pattern.

BOY: Fresh newspaper cut in fancy-edge on the kitchen shelves.

MAN: The front door stood open to the sunshine so that the floor of the front room could finish drying after its weekly scouring.

WOMAN: Missie May . . .

(*The* BOY *lowers a "theatrical curtain" to reveal* MISSIE MAY, *as if she were bathing.*)

WOMAN: Was bathing herself in the galvanized washtub in the bedroom. Her dark-brown skin . . .

MISSIE: Glistened . . .

WOMAN: Under the soapsuds that skittered down from her wash rag. Her stiff young breasts . . .

MISSIE: Thrust forward aggressively . . .

WOMAN: Like broad-based cones with tips lacquered in black.

MISSIE: She heard men's voices in the distance and glanced at the dollar clock on the dresser.

Humph! Ah'm way behind time t'day! Joe gointer be heah 'fore Ah git my clothes on if Ah don't make haste.

She grabbed the clean meal sack at hand and dried herself hurriedly and began to dress.

(*The* MAN *heralds the entrance of* JOE.)

MISSIE: But before she could tie her slippers, there came the ring of singing metal on wood . . .

(*As* JOE *hurls the coins, the* WOMAN *produces the sound of the falling coins by shaking a tambourine.*)

MISSIE: Nine times!

JOE: Missie grinned with delight. She had not seen the big tall man come stealing in the gate and creep up the walk grinning happily at the joyful mischief he was about to commit.

MISSIE: But she knew it was her husband throwing silver dollars in the door for her to pick up and pile beside her plate at dinner. It was this way every Saturday afternoon.

JOE: The nine dollars hurled into the open door, he scurried to a hiding place behind the cape jasmine bush and waited.

(*The* BOY *lifts a branch, bursting with flowers, thereby becoming a tree, which* JOE *hides behind.*)

MISSIE: Missie promptly appeared at the door in mock alarm. (*Calling out*) Who dat chunkin' money in mah do'way?

She leaped off the porch and began to search the shrubbery.

JOE: While she did this, the man behind the jasmine darted to the chinaberry tree.

MISSIE: She peeped under the porch and hung over the gate to look up and down the road. She spied him and gave chase. (*Calling out*) Ain't nobody gointer be chunkin' money at me and Ah not do'em nothin'.

(*As the chase between* MISSIE *and* JOE *ensues . . .*)

MAN: He ran around the house, Missie May at his heels.

WOMAN: She overtook him at the kitchen door.

BOY: He ran inside but could not close it after him before she . . .

WOMAN: Crowded in and locked with him in a rough and tumble.

MAN: For several minutes the two were a furious mass of male and female energy.

WOMAN: Shouting!

MAN: Laughing!

BOY: Twisting!

WOMAN: Turning!

BOY: Joe trying but not too hard to get away.

JOE: Missie May, take yo' hand outta mah pocket.

MISSIE: Ah ain't, Joe, not lessen you gwine gimme whateve' it is good you got in yo' pocket. Turn it go Joe, do Ah'll tear yo' clothes.

JOE: Go on tear 'em. You de one dat pushes de needles round heah. Move yo' hand Missie May.

MISSIE: Lemme git that paper sack out yo' pocket. Ah bet it's candy kisses.

JOE: Tain't. Move yo' hand. Woman ain't got no business in a man's clothes nohow. Go 'way.

MISSIE: Missie May gouged way down and gave an upward jerk and triumphed.

Unhhunh! Ah got it. And it 'tis so candy kisses. Ah knowed you had somethin' for me in yo' clothes. Now Ah got to see whut's in every pocket you got.

JOE: Joe smiled . . . and let his wife go through all of his pockets and take out the things that he had hidden there for her to find.

WOMAN: She bore off the chewing gum. The cake of sweet soap. The pocket handkerchief . . .

BOY: As if she had wrested them from him . . .

MAN: As if they had not been bought for the sake of this friendly battle.

GUITAR MAN/PLAYERS:
YOUR LOVE HAS SHOOK ME UP
AND IT BRINGS OUT THE BOOGIE IN ME
YOUR LOVE HAS SHOOK ME UP
AND IT BRINGS OUT THE BOOGIE IN ME
YOUR LOVE HAS SHOOK ME UP
AND IT BRINGS OUT THE BOOGIE IN ME

(*Music underscore ends. The* PLAYERS *are gone and* MISSIE *and* JOE *are alone. The energy between them changes; from frolicsome to seductive.*)

JOE: Whew! That play-fight done got me all warmed up. Got me some water in de kittle?

MISSIE: Yo' water is on de fire and yo' clean things is cross de bed. Hurry up and wash yo'self and git changed so we kin eat. Ah'm hongry.

JOE: You ain't hongry sugar. Youse jes's little empty. Ah'm de one with all the hongry. Ah could eat up camp meetin', back off 'ssociation and drink Jurdan dry. You have it on de table when Ah git out de tub.

MISSIE: Don't you mess wid my business, man. Ah'm a real wife, not no dress and breath. Ah might not look lak one, but if you burn me down, you won't git a thing but wife ashes.

   Joe splashed in the bedroom and Missie May fanned around in the kitchen. A fresh red and white checked cloth on the table. Big pitcher of buttermilk beaded with pale drops of butter from the churn. Hot fried mullet.

JOE (*Elated*): Huh?

MISSIE: Crackling bread.

JOE: Ummm?

MISSIE: Ham hocks atop a mound of string beans and new potatoes.

JOE: Ummmm.

MISSIE: And perched on the window-sill . . .

JOE/MISSIE: A pone of spicy potato pudding.

(*Lights reveal the* PLAYERS.)

MAN: Very little talk during the meal . . .

(*The* BOY *presents a tray containing a plate of food, which he places before* MISSIE *and* JOE.)

BOY: Except banter that pretended to deny affection . . .
WOMAN: But in reality flaunted it.

(*The* BOY *flips the tray to reveal a plate containing dessert.*)

JOE (*As if he's just eaten a full meal*): Ummmm. We goin' down de road a li'l piece t'night so go put on yo' Sunday-go-to-meetin' things.
MISSIE: Sho' nuff, Joe?
JOE: Yeah. A new man done come heah from Chicago. Got a place and took and opened it up for an ice cream parlor, and bein' as it's real swell, Ah wants you to be one of de first ladies to walk in dere and have some set down.
MISSIE: Do Jesus, Ah ain't knowed nothin' 'bout it. Who de man done it?
JOE: Mister Otis D. Slemmons, of spots and places.

(*Lights reveal the* MAN, *playing the role of* SLEMMONS. *Hanging from his vest, gold coins on a chain. Music underscore.*)

SLEMMONS: Memphis, Chicago, Jacksonville, Philadelphia and so on.
MISSIE: You mean that heavy-set man wid his mouth full of gold teethes?
JOE: Yeah. Where did you see 'im at?
MISSIE: Ah went down to de sto' tuh git a box of lye and Ah seen 'im.
SLEMMONS: Standin' on de corner talkin' to some of de mens.
MISSIE: And Ah come on back and went to scrubbin' de floor, and whilst I was scouring the steps . . .
SLEMMONS: He passed and tipped his hat.
MISSIE: And Ah thought, hmmm, never Ah seen him before.
JOE: Yeah, he's up to date.
SLEMMONS: He got de finest clothes Ah ever seen on a colored man's back.
MISSIE: Aw, he don't look no better in his clothes than you do in yourn. He got a puzzlegut on 'im. And he's so chuckle-headed, he got a pone behind his neck.

JOE: He ain't puzzle-gutted honey. He jes' got a corperation. That make 'm look lak a rich white man. Wisht Ah had a build on me lak he got.

SLEMMONS: All rich mens got some belly on 'em.

MISSIE: Ah seen de pitchers of Henry Ford and he's a spare-built man. And Rockefeller look lak he ain't got but one gut. But Ford, Rockefeller and dis Slemmons and all de rest kin be as many-gutted as dey please. Ah'm satisfied wid you jes' like you is, baby. God took pattern after a pine tree and built you noble. Youse a pretty still man. And if Ah knowed any way to make you mo' pritty still, Ah'd take and do it.

(*They kiss.*)

JOE: You jes' say dat cause you love me. But Ah know Ah can't hold no light to Otis D. Slemmons. Ah ain't never been no-where and Ah ain't got nothin' but you.

MISSIE: How you know dat, Joe.

JOE: He tole us so hisself.

(SLEMMONS *moves in and around the scene, his presence never acknowledged by* MISSIE *or* JOE.)

MISSIE: Dat don't make it so. His mouf is cut cross-ways ain't it? Well, he kin lie jes' like anybody else.

JOE: Good Lawd, Missie! He's got a five-dollar gold piece for a stick-pin.

SLEMMONS: And a ten-dollar gold piece for his watch chain.

JOE: And his mouf is jes' crammed full of gold teeth. And whut make it so cool, he got money 'cumulated.

SLEMMONS: And womens give it all to 'im.

MISSIE: Ah don't see whut de womens sees on 'im. Ah wouldn't give 'im a wind if de sherff wuz after 'im.

JOE: Well, he tole us how de white womens in Chicago give 'im all dat gold money.

SLEMMONS: So he don't 'low nobody to touch it. Not even put dey finger on it at all.

JOE: You can make 'miration at it, but don't tetch it.

MISSIE: Whyn't he stay up dere where dey so crazy 'bout 'im?

JOE: Ah reckon dey done make 'im vast-rich and he wants to travel some. He say dey wouldn't leave 'im hit a lick of work.

SLEMMONS: He got mo' lady people crazy 'bout him than he kin shake a stick at.

MISSIE: Joe, Ah hates to see you so dumb. Dat stray nigger jes' tell y'all anything and y'all b'lieve it.

JOE: Go 'head on now, honey and put on yo' clothes. He talkin' 'bout his pritty womens—Ah wants 'im to see mine.

MISSIE: Missie May went off to dress.

(*As* MISSIE *exits, the music fades.*)

JOE (*Confidentially to the audience*): And Joe spent the time trying to make his stomach punch out like Slemmons' middle.

MAN: But found that his tall bone-and-muscle stride fitted ill with it.

(*Music underscore. The* MAN *"becomes"* SLEMMONS *and the playing arena, a juke joint.* GUITAR MAN *and the* WOMAN *are on hand as the entertainment.*)

SLEMMONS: Hey yaw! Welcome to Otis D. Slemmons Ice Creme Parlor and Fun House!

(*As* GUITAR MAN/WOMAN *sing,* JOE *and* MISSIE *enter the Parlor. He introduces* MISSIE *to* SLEMMONS *and then grabs her and begins to dance.*)

SONG: TELL ME MAMA

GUITAR MAN/WOMAN:
TELL ME MAMA,
WHAT IS WRONG WITH YOU
    (TELL ME MAMA, WON'TCHA TELL ME
        MAMA)
TELL ME MAMA,
WHAT IS WRONG WITH YOU
    (TELL ME MAMA, WON'TCHA TELL
        ME MAMA)
YOU MUST WANT SOMEBODY
TO LAY DOWN AND DIE FOR YOU

IT RAINED FORTY DAYS
FORTY NIGHTS WITHOUT STOPPIN'
    (JONAH)

JONAH GOT MAD CAUSE
THE RAIN KEPT ON DROPPIN'
   (JONAH)
JONAH RUN AND GOT
IN THE BELLY OF THE WHALE
   (JONAH)
NINETY TIMES I'M GON'
TELL THAT SAME BIG TALE

THE WHALE BEGAN TO WIGGLE
   (JONAH)
JONAH BEGAN TO SCRATCH
   (JONAH)
THE WHALE GO JUMP
IN SOMEONE'S SWEET POTATO PATCH

OH TELL ME MAMA,
WHAT IS WRONG WITH YOU
  (TELL ME MAMA, WON'TCHA TELL
    ME MAMA)
TELL ME MAMA
WHAT IS WRONG WITH YOU
  (TELL ME MAMA, WON'TCHA TELL
    ME MAMA)
YOU MUST WANT SOMEBODY
TO LAY DOWN AND DIE FOR YOU

(JOE, *caught up in the music, doesn't notice* SLEMMONS *has grabbed his wife and is now dancing with her.* MISSIE *is clearly mesmerized by* SLEMMONS' *"gold."*)

GUITAR MAN/WOMAN:
TWO CHEAP EASY MORGAN,
RUNNIN' SIDE BY SIDE

(*Everybody adds in.*)

ALL:
TWO CHEAP EASY MORGAN
RUNNIN' SIDE BY SIDE
IF YOU CATCH YO'SELF A CHEAPY
THEY MIGHT AS WELL LET YOU RIDE

IF YOU CATCH YO'SELF A CHEAPY
THEY MIGHT AS WELL LET YOU RIDE

IF YOU CATCH YO'SELF A CHEAPY
THEY MIGHT AS WELL LET YOU . . .
RIDE!

(*The number ends. The* PLAYERS *watch the scene between* JOE *and* MISSIE.)

JOE: Didn't Ah say ole Otis was swell? Can't he talk Chicago talk? And know what he tole me when Ah was payin' for our ice cream? He say—

(*The* MAN *becomes* SLEMMONS.)

SLEMMONS: Ah have to hand it to you, Joe. Dat wife of yours is jes' thirty-eight and two. Yessuh, she's forty shakes!
JOE: Ain't he killin'?
MISSIE: He'll do in case of a rush. But he sho' is got uh heap uh gold on 'im. Dat's de first time Ah ever seed gold money. It lookted good on him sho' nuff, but it'd look a whole heap better on you.
JOE: Who me? Missie May was youse crazy! Where would a po' man lak me git gold money from?
WOMAN: Missie May was silent for a minute.
BOY (*Overlapping*): Missie May was silent for a minute.
MAN (*Overlapping*): Missie May was silent for a minute.
MISSIE: Us might find some goin' long de road some time.

(JOE *laughs.*)

MISSIE: Us could!
JOE (*Laughing*): Who would be losin' gold money 'round heah? We ain't ever seen none of dese white folks wearin' no gold money on dey watch chain.
MISSIE: You don't know whut been lost 'round heah. Maybe somebody way back in memorial times lost they gold money and went on off and it ain't never been found. And then if we wuz to find it, you could wear some 'thout havin' no gang of womens lak dat Slemmons say he got.

JOE: Don't be so wishful 'bout me. Ah'm satisfied de way Ah is. So long as Ah be yo' husband, Ah don't keer 'bout nothin' else. Ah'd ruther all the other womens in de world to be dead then for you to have de toothache. (*He kisses her*) Less we go to bed and git our night's rest.

(*Music underscore. As* MAN *and* WOMAN *speak, the* BOY *holds a fall branch, under which* MISSIE *and* JOE *dance—their moves sensuous.*)

MAN: It was Saturday night once more before Joe could parade his wife in Slemmons' ice cream parlor.

BOY: He worked the night shift and Saturday was his only night off.

WOMAN: Every other evening around six o'clock he left home and dying dawn saw him hustling home around the lake.

MAN: That was the best part of life . . .

WOMAN: Going home to Missie May.

MAN: Their whitewashed house . . .

WOMAN: Their mock battle on Saturday . . .

MAN: Dinner and ice cream parlor afterwards . . .

WOMAN: Church on Sunday nights when Missie outdressed any woman in town.

(JOE *kisses* MISSIE *goodbye.*)

JOE (*To the audience*): Everything was right!

MAN: One night around eleven the acid ran out at the G and G.

BOY: The foreman knocked off the crew and let the steam die down.

(*Lights isolate* JOE. *During the following sequence the* MAN *and* BOY *become the voices in* JOE'S *head, his feelings; at times even becoming* JOE, *mirroring his moves. Even though* MISSIE *is discussed, she is not seen during this sequence.*)

JOE: As Joe rounded the lake on his way home . . .

WOMAN:

A LEAN MOON RODE THE LAKE ON A SILVER BOAT.

MAN: If anybody had asked Joe about the moon on the lake, he would have said he hadn't paid it any attention.

JOE: But he saw it with his feelings. It made him yearn painfully for Missie May.

BOY: Missie May.

JOE: They had been married for more than a year now. They had money put away. They ought to be making little feet for shoes. A little boy child would be about right.

MAN: Be about right.

BOY: He saw a dim light in the bedroom . . .

MAN: And decided to come in through the kitchen door.

JOE: He could wash the fertilizer dust off himself before presenting himself to Missie May. It would be nice for her not to know that he was there until he slipped into his place in bed and hugged her back.

JOE/BOY/MAN: She always liked that!

BOY: He eased the kitchen door open . . .

JOE: Slowly and silently . . .

MAN: But when he went to set his dinner bucket on the table—

JOE: He bumped.

BOY: Into a pile of dishes.

MAN: And something crashed to the floor.

JOE: He heard his wife gasp in fright and hurried to reassure her. (*A hushed voice*) Iss me, honey. Don't get skeered.

MAN: There was a quick large movement in the bedroom.

BOY: A rustle.

MAN: A thud.

BOY: A stealthy silence.

MAN: The lights went out.

JOE (*After a beat*): What?

BOY: Robbers?

MAN: Murderers?

BOY: Someone attacking your helpless wife, perhaps?

JOE: He struck a match, threw himself on guard and stepped over the door-sill into the bedroom.

WOMAN: The great belt on the wheel of Time slipped. And eternity stood still.

MAN: By the match light he could see . . .

JOE: The man's legs fighting with his breeches in his frantic desire to get them on.

BOY: He had both chance and time to kill the intruder.

JOE: But he was too weak to take action. He was assaulted in his weakness.

MAN: Like Samson awakening after his haircut.

BOY: So he just opened his mouth . . .

JOE: And laughed.

MAN: The match went out.

BOY: He struck another.

MAN: And lit the lamp.

JOE: A howling wind raced across his heart.

MAN AND BOY (*Echoing*): His heart . . . his heart.

JOE: But underneath its fury he heard his wife sobbing.

MAN: And Slemmons pleading for his life. Offering to buy it with all that he had. (*As Slemmons*) Please suh, don't kill me. Sixty-two dollars at de sto' gold money.

JOE: Joe just stood there.

MAN: Slemmons considered a surprise attack.

BOY: But before his fist could travel an inch . . .

JOE: Joe's own rushed out to crush him like a battering ram. Git into yo' damn rags Slemmons and dat quick!

MAN: Slemmons scrambled to his feet.

JOE: He grabbed at him with his left hand and struck at him with his right.

MAN: Slemmons was knocked into the kitchen and fled through the front door.

(*Music underscore ends.*)

WOMAN: Joe found himself alone with Missie May, the golden watch charm clutched in his left hand. A short bit of broken chain dangled between his fingers.

(*In isolated light,* MISSIE *and* JOE, *as the* PLAYERS *look on.*)

MISSIE: Missie May was sobbing.

JOE (*Simultaneously*): Joe stood and stood.

MISSIE: Wails of weeping without words . . .

JOE (*Simultaneously*): And felt without thinking . . . and without seeing with his natural eyes Joe kept on . . .

MISSIE: She kept on crying . . .

JOE (*Simultaneously*): . . . feeling so much and not knowing what to do with all his feelings.
    Missie May whut you cryin' for?

MISSIE: Cause Ah love you so hard and Ah know you don't love me no mo'.

JOE: You don't know de feelings of dat yet, Missie May.

MISSIE: Oh Joe, honey, he said he was gointer gimme dat gold money and he jes' kept on after me.

JOE: Well don't cry no mo' Miss May. Ah got yo' gold piece for you.

He put Slemmons' watch charm in his pants pocket and went to bed.

(*Music underscore.*)

MAN: The hours went past. Joe still and quiet on one bed rail.

BOY: And Miss May wrung dry of sobs on the other.

WOMAN:
FINALLY THE SUN'S TIDE
CREPT UPON THE SHORE OF NIGHT
AND DROWNED ALL ITS HOURS

MISSIE: Missie May with her face stiff and streaked towards the window saw the dawn come into her yard. It was day, nothing more. Joe wouldn't be coming home as usual. No need to fling open the front door and sweep off the porch, making it nice for Joe. No more breakfast to cook; no more washing and starching of Joe's jumper-jackets and pants. No more nothing.

JOE: No more nothing.

MISSIE: So why get up. With this strange man in her bed, Missie felt embarrassed to get up and dress. She decided to wait till he had dressed and gone. Then she would get up, dress quickly and be gone forever beyond reach of Joe's looks and laughs. But he never moved.

JOE: He never moved.

MISSIE: Red light turned to yellow, then white.

WOMAN: From beyond the no-man's land between them came a voice.

(*Music underscore ends.*)

MAN: A strange voice that yesterday had been Joe's.

JOE: Missie May ain't you gonna fix me no breakfus'?

MISSIE: She sprang out of bed.

Yeah Joe. Ah didn't reckon you wuz hongry.

No need to die today. Joe needed her for a few more minutes anyhow.

WOMAN: Soon there was a roaring fire in the cook stove.

MAN: Water bucket full and two chickens killed.

BOY: She rushed hot biscuits to the table as Joe took his seat.

JOE: He ate with his eyes on his plate.

WOMAN: No laughter, no banter.

JOE: Missie May you ain't eatin' yo' breakfus'?

MISSIE: Ah don't choose none, Ah thank yuh.

JOE: His coffee cup was empty.

MISSIE: She sprang to refill it.

BOY: When she turned from the stove and bent to set the cup
beside Joe's plate, she saw . . .

MISSIE: The yellow coin on the table between them.

GUITAR MAN/PLAYERS:

THE SUN CAME UP
AND THE SUN WENT DOWN
THE SUN CAME UP
AND THE SUN WENT DOWN

(GUITAR MAN *maintains the above chant as isolated pools of light
reveal* MISSIE *and* JOE. *The* PLAYERS *chronicle the passage of time
with their movements.*)

WOMAN: The sun, the hero of every day, the impersonal old man
that beams as brightly on death as on birth, came up every
morning and raced across the blue dome and dipped into the
sea of fire every evening.

MAN: Water ran down hill.

BOY: Birds nested.

WOMAN: But there were no more Saturday romps.

MAN: No ringing silver dollars to stack beside her plate.

MISSIE: No pockets to rifle.

WOMAN: In fact the yellow coin in his trousers was like a monster
hiding in the cave of his pockets to destroy her.

MAN: She often wondered if he still had it but nothing could have
induced her to ask nor explore his pockets to see for herself.

BOY: Its shadow was in the house whether or no.

GUITAR MAN/PLAYERS:

THE SUN CAME UP
AND THE SUN WENT DOWN

THE SUN CAME UP
AND THE SUN WENT DOWN

MISSIE: She knew why she didn't leave Joe. She couldn't. She loved
him too much. But she couldn't understand why Joe didn't
leave her. He was polite, even kind at times, but aloof.

GUITAR MAN/PLAYERS:
THE SUN CAME UP
AND THE SUN WENT DOWN
THE SUN CAME UP
AND THE SUN WENT DOWN

MAN: One night Joe came home around midnight . . .

JOE: Complained of pains in the back. He asked Missie to rub him
down with liniment.

MISSIE: It had been three months since Missie had touched his body
and it all seemed strange. But she rubbed him. Grateful for the
chance.

JOE: Before morning, youth triumphed . . .

MISSIE: And Missie exulted.

GUITAR MAN/PLAYERS:
THE SUN CAME UP
AND THE SUN WENT DOWN
THE SUN CAME UP
AND THE SUN WENT DOWN

BOY: But the next day beneath her pillow she found . . .

MISSIE: The piece of money with the bit of chain attached.

WOMAN: She took it into her hands with trembling and saw first
that it was no gold piece.

MAN: It was a gilded half-dollar.

MISSIE: Then she knew why Slemmons had forbidden anyone to
touch his gold.

WOMAN: He trusted village eyes at a distance not to recognize his
stick-pin as a gilded quarter.

BOY: And his watch charm as a four-bit piece.

MISSIE: She was glad at first that Joe had left it there. Perhaps he
was through with her punishment. They were man and wife
again.

MAN: Then another thought came clawing at her.

MISSIE: He had come home to buy from her as if she were any
woman in the long house. As if to say that he could pay as well
as Slemmons. She slid the coin into his Sunday pants pocket and

dressed herself and left his house. Halfway between her house and the quarters, she met her husband's mother . . .

(MISSIE *finds herself trapped in the severe gaze of the* WOMAN *who has "become"* JOE's *mother.*)

MISSIE: And after a short talk she turned and went back home. If she had not the substance of marriage, she had the outside show. Joe must leave *her*. She let him see she didn't want his old gold four-bits too.

GUITAR MAN/PLAYERS:
THE SUN CAME UP
AND THE SUN WENT DOWN
THE SUN CAME UP
AND THE SUN WENT DOWN

MISSIE: She saw no more of the coin for some time though she knew that Joe could not help finding it in his pocket. But his health kept poor . . .

JOE: And he came home at least every ten days . . .

MISSIE: To be rubbed.

GUITAR MAN:
THE SUN WENT DOWN
THE SUN CAME UP
THE SUN WENT DOWN

WOMAN:
THE SUN SWEPT AROUND THE HORIZON
TRAILING ITS ROBES OF WEEKS AND DAYS

GUITAR MAN:
THE SUN CAME UP.

(*The* WOMAN *tosses snow into the air as the* BOY *lifts a barren branch. It is now winter. Music underscore ends as* JOE *stands before a very pregnant* MISSIE.)

JOE: One morning Joe came in from work, he found Missie May chopping wood. Without a word he took the ax and chopped a huge pile before he stopped. (*To* MISSIE) You ain't got no business choppin' wood and you know it.

MISSIE: How come? Ah been choppin' it for de last longest.

JOE: Ah ain't blind. You makin' feet for shoes.

MISSIE: Won't you be glad to have a li'l baby child Joe?

JOE: You know dat 'thout astin' me.

MISSIE: Iss gointer be a boy chile and de very spit of you.

JOE: You reckon Missie May?

MISSIE: Who else could it look lak?

JOE: Joe said nothing.

MISSIE: But thrust his hand deep into his pocket and fingered something.

(*Music underscore.*)

MAN: It was almost three months later Missie May took to bed.

BOY: And Joe went and got his mother to come wait on the house.

(*Lights reveal* MISSIE *and the* WOMAN, *as* JOE's *mother, assisting* MISSIE *as she gives birth. The* WOMAN *hums/moans* MISSIE's *pain, which builds to a gospel wail, until . . .*)

WOMAN: Missie May delivered a fine boy.

(*Music underscore ends.*)

BOY: When Joe came in from work one morning—

MAN: His mother and the old women were drinking great bowls of coffee around the fire in the kitchen.

(JOE *crosses to his mother. The* MAN *looks on.*)

JOE: How did Missie May make out?

MOTHER: Who, dat gal? She strong as a ox. She gointer have plenty mo'. We done fixed her wid de sugar and lard to sweeten her for de nex' one.

MAN: Joe stood silent.

MOTHER: You ain't ast 'bout de baby Joe. You oughter be mighty proud cause he sho' is de spittin' image of yuh, son. Dat's yourn all right, if you never git another one, dat un is yourn.

(JOE *grabs his mother, hugs her, lets out a shout.*)

MOTHER: And you know Ah'm mighty proud too, son, cause Ah never thought well of you marryin' Missie May cause her ma used tuh fan her foot 'round right smart and Ah been mighty

skeered dat Missie May wuz gointer git misput on her road.
Bless you son.

(*She exits.*)

JOE: Joe said nothing.

(*Music underscore.*)

JOE: He fooled around the house till late in the day then just
before he went to work, he went and stood at the foot of the
bed and asked his wife how she felt.
MISSIE: He did this every day during the week.
WOMAN: On Saturday he went to Orlando to make his market.
MAN: Way after while he went around to the candy store.

(*The* BOY *appears as the clerk, his voice, manner and the mask he
wears suggestive of a "Southern Cracker."*)

CLERK: Hello Joe, the clerk greeted him. Ain't seen you in a long
time.
JOE: Nope. Ah ain't been heah. Been 'round spots and places.
CLERK: Want some of them molasses kisses you always buy?
JOE: Yessuh. Will this spend?
CLERK: Whut is it Joe? Well I'll be doggone! A gold-plated four-bit
piece. Where'd you git it Joe?
JOE: Offen a stray nigger dat come through Eatonville. He had it
on his watch chain for a charm—goin' 'round making out iss
gold money. Ha ha! He had a quarter on his tie pin and it wuz
all golded up too. Tryin' to fool people. Makin' out he so rich
and everything. Tryin' to tole off folkses wives from home.
CLERK: How did you git it Joe? Did he fool you too?
JOE: Who me? Naw suh! He ain't fooled me none. Know whut Ah
done? He come 'round wid his smart talk and Ah hauled off
and knocked 'im down and took his old four-bits 'way from 'im.
Gointer buy my wife some good ole 'lasses kisses wid it. Gimme
fifty cents worth of dem candy kisses.
CLERK: Fifty cents buy a mightly lot of candy kisses, Joe. Why
don't you split it up and take some chocolate bars, too. They eat
good, too.

JOE: Yessuh, dey do, but Ah wants all dat in kisses. Ah got a li'l boy chile home now. Tain't a week old yet, but he kin suck a sugar tit and maybe eat one them kisses hisself.

CLERK: Joe got his candy and left the store. The clerk turned to the next customer.

Wisht I could be like these darkies. Laughin' all the time. Nothin' worries 'em.

(*The* MAN, WOMAN *and* BOY *each make grand entrances, signaling the story is about to end.*)

MAN: Back in Eatonville . . .

WOMAN: Joe reached his own front door.

BOY: There was a ring of singing metal on wood.

(*As* JOE *tosses the coins, the* WOMAN *shakes the tambourine.*)

JOE: Fifteen times!

MISSIE: Missie May couldn't run to the door, but she crept there as quickly as she could.

Joe Banks, Ah hear you chunkin' money in mah do'way. You wait till Ah got mah strength back and Ah'm gointer fix you for dat.

GUITAR MAN:
THE SUN CAME UP

PLAYERS:
I GIT TO THE GIT

GUITAR MAN:
THE SUN WENT DOWN

PLAYERS:
WITH SOME PAIN N' SOME SPIT
N' SOME . . .

GUITAR MAN:
THE SUN CAME UP.

PLAYERS:
SPUNK.

(*On the word "spunk,"* MISSIE *and* JOE *kiss, their figures cast in silhouette. The* MAN *gestures. The tale has ended. Blackout.*)

END OF PLAY

GLOSSARY FOR "STORY IN HARLEM SLANG"

AIR OUT: leave, flee, stroll.

ASTORPERIOUS: haughty, biggity.

'BAM, DOWN IN 'BAM: down South.

BEATING UP YOUR GUMS: talking to no purpose.

BULL-SKATING: bragging.

COLLAR A NOD: sleep.

COAL-SCUTTLE BLOND: black woman.

CUT: doing something well.

DIDDY-WAH-DIDDY: (1) a far place, a measure of distance; (2) another suburb of Hell, built since way before Hell wasn't no bigger than Baltimore. The folks in Hell go there for a big time.

DUMB TO THE FACT: "You don't know what you're talking about."

FRAIL EEL: pretty girl.

GINNY GALL: a suburb of Hell, a long way off.

GRANNY GRUNT: a mythical character to whom most questions may be referred.

I DON'T DEAL IN COAL: "I don't keep company with black women."

JIG: Negro, a corrupted shortening of Zigaboo.

JELLY: sex.

JULY JAM: something very hot.

JUMP SALTY: get angry.

KITCHEN MECHANIC: a domestic.

MANNY: a term of insult; never used in any other way by Negroes.

MISS ANNE: a white woman.

MY PEOPLE! MY PEOPLE!: sad and satiric expression in the Negro language; sad when a Negro comments on the backwardness of some members of his race; at other times, used for satiric or comic effect.

PE-OLA: a very white Negro girl.

PIANO: spareribs (white rib bones suggest piano keys).

PLAYING THE DOZENS: low-rating the ancestors of your opponent.

REEFER: a marijuana cigarette, also a drag.

RIGHTEOUS MOSS OR GRASS: good hair.

RUSSIAN: a southern Negro up North. "Rushed up here," hence a Russian.

SCRAP-IRON: cheap liquor.

SOLID: perfect.

STANCH or STANCH OUT: to begin, commence, step out.

SUGAR HILL: northwest sector of Harlem, near Washington Heights; site of the newest apartment houses, mostly occupied by professional people. (The expression has been distorted in the South to mean a Negro red-light district.)

THE BEAR: confession of poverty.

THOUSAND ON A PLATE: beans.

WHAT'S ON DE RAIL FOR THE LIZARD?: suggestion for moral turpitude.

ZIGABOO: a Negro.

ZOOT SUIT WITH THE REET PLEAT: Harlem-style suit with padded shoulders, 43-inch trousers at the knee with cuff so small it needs a zipper to get into, high waistline, fancy lapels, bushels of buttons, etc.

MUSIC

Jurden Water

DELIA,
ENSEMBLE AND
ACOUSTIC GUITAR

BY CHIC STREET MAN

I've Been Livin' with the Blues

GUITAR MAN
AND ACOUSTIC GUITAR

ARRANGED BY
CHIC STREET MAN

Hey Lady

GUITAR MAN,
BLUES SPEAK WOMAN
AND ACOUSTIC GUITAR

BY CHIC STREET MAN

-LY   SLIGHT- LY ___   AND OOH SO PO-LITE-

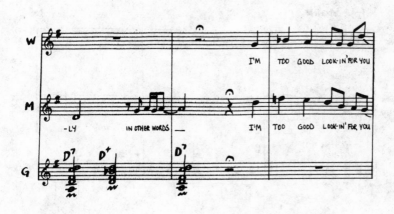

W: I'M TOO GOOD LOOK-IN' FOR YOU

M: -LY   IN OTHER WORDS ___   I'M TOO GOOD LOOK-IN' FOR YOU

BOTH: But then again...

You Brings out the Boogie in Me

BLUES SPEAK WOMAN,
GUITAR MAN AND
ACOUSTIC GUITAR

ARRANGED BY
CHIC STREET MAN

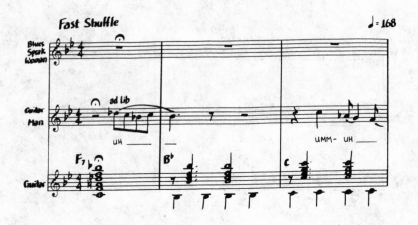

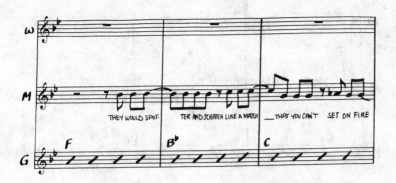

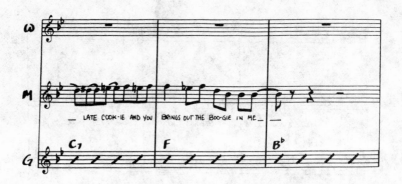

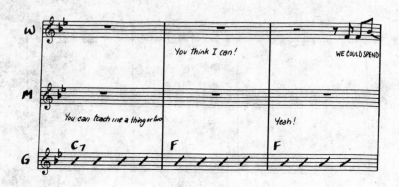

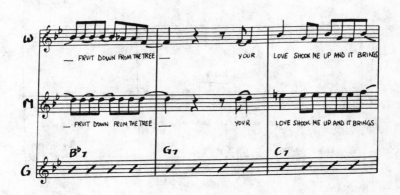

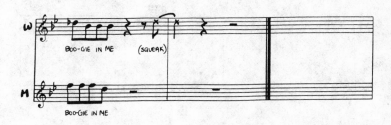

Tell Me Mama!

GUITAR MAN,
HARMONICA AND
ACOUSTIC GUITAR

ARRANGED BY
CHIC STREET MAN

TELL ME MA-MA WHAT IS WRONG WITH YOU

SO TELL ME MA—MA— WHAT— IS— WRONG— WITH YOU

YOU MUST WANT SOME-BO-DY TO LAY

DOWN AND DIE FOR YOU— — LORD TWO— CHEAP— EA-—

—SY— MOR—GAN— RUN-NIN' SIDE BY SIDE—

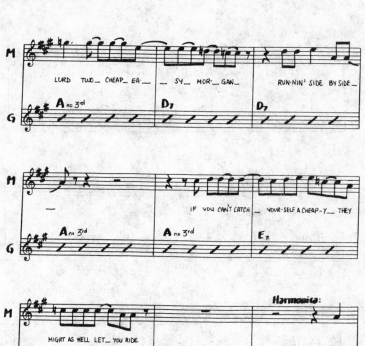

LORD TWO_ CHEAP_ EA·_ _ SY_ MOR·_ GAN_   RUN-NIN' SIDE BY SIDE_

A no 3rd   D7   D7

_   IF YOU CAN'T CATCH _ YOUR-SELF A CHEAP-Y_ THEY

A no 3rd   A no 3rd   E7

Harmonica:

MIGHT AS WELL LET_ YOU RIDE

E7   A   A

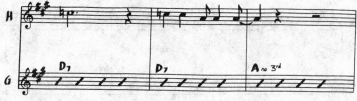

D7   D7   A no 3rd

A no 3rd   D7   D7

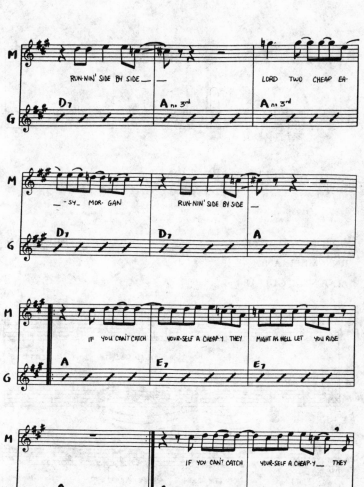
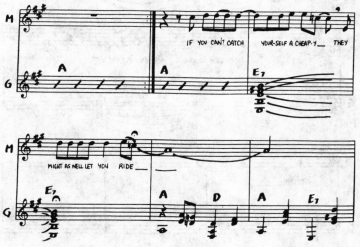

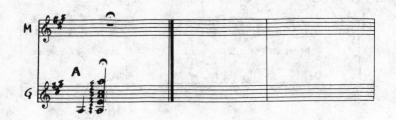

Spunk Tag

GUITAR MAN,
ENSEMBLE AND
ACOUSTIC GUITAR

BY CHIC STREET MAN

ABOUT THE AUTHOR

Zora Neale Hurston (1903–1960), novelist, dramatist and folklorist, was born and raised in Eatonville, Florida, the first incorporated all-black town in America. She attended Howard University in Washington, D.C. and studied anthropology with Franz Boas at both Barnard College and Columbia University in New York City. Anthropological researches in her native South provided the basis for all of her writings, which were and remain extremely controversial due to their unflinching—some would say stereotypical—portrayal of African Americans.

Despite early success and a close association with the artists of the Harlem Renaissance, Hurston died poor and forgotten. Rediscovery in the seventies by feminist scholars and writers has led to a fuller appreciation of her standing in American letters and burgeoning production and publication activities.

Her major works include the novel *Their Eyes Were Watching God* and an autobiography, *Dust Tracks on a Road*.

ABOUT THE COMPOSER

Chic Street Man is a singer, songwriter and musical Ambassador for Peace and Human Rights. He has recorded and toured throughout France and other parts of Europe and directed and toured with two *Peace Child* shows to the Soviet Union. He works with children and adults through his workshop in the performing arts to build self-confidence and self-esteem and recently appeared in concert at the General Assembly of the United Nations.